ROUTLEDGE LIBRARY EDITIONS: SCOTLAND

Volume 20

SCOTLAND'S ECONOMIC PROGRESS 1951–1960

SCOTLAND'S ECONOMIC PROGRESS 1951–1960

A Study in Regional Accounting

GAVIN McCRONE

LONDON AND NEW YORK

First published in 1965 by George Allen & Unwin Ltd

This edition first published in 2022
by Routledge
2 Park Square, Milton Park, Abingdon, Oxon OX14 4RN

and by Routledge
605 Third Avenue, New York, NY 10158

Routledge is an imprint of the Taylor & Francis Group, an informa business

© 1965 George Allen & Unwin Ltd

All rights reserved. No part of this book may be reprinted or reproduced or utilised in any form or by any electronic, mechanical, or other means, now known or hereafter invented, including photocopying and recording, or in any information storage or retrieval system, without permission in writing from the publishers.

Trademark notice: Product or corporate names may be trademarks or registered trademarks, and are used only for identification and explanation without intent to infringe.

British Library Cataloguing in Publication Data
A catalogue record for this book is available from the British Library

ISBN: 978-1-03-206184-9 (Set)
ISBN: 978-1-00-321338-3 (Set) (ebk)
ISBN: 978-1-03-207687-4 (Volume 20) (hbk)
ISBN: 978-1-03-207704-8 (Volume 20) (pbk)
ISBN: 978-1-00-320840-2 (Volume 20) (ebk)

DOI: 10.4324/9781003208402

Publisher's Note
The publisher has gone to great lengths to ensure the quality of this reprint but points out that some imperfections in the original copies may be apparent.

Disclaimer
The publisher has made every effort to trace copyright holders and would welcome correspondence from those they have been unable to trace.

SCOTLAND'S ECONOMIC PROGRESS
1951-1960
A Study in Regional Accounting

BY

GAVIN MCCRONE

London
GEORGE ALLEN & UNWIN LTD
RUSKIN HOUSE   MUSEUM STREET

FIRST PUBLISHED IN 1965

This book is copyright under the Berne Convention. Apart from any fair dealing for the purposes of private study, research, criticism or review, as permitted under the Copyright Act, 1956, no portion may be reproduced by any process without written permission. Enquiry should be made to the publishers

© *George Allen & Unwin Ltd, 1965*

PRINTED IN GREAT BRITAIN
in 10 point Times Roman type
BY SIMSON SHAND LTD
LONDON, HERTFORD AND HARLOW

PREFACE

MY greatest debt in writing this book is to the authors of previous studies on regional economic statistics. From their work I have learnt much which made the task of preparing the estimates in this book incomparably easier. In particular I derived great advantage from reading three dissertations submitted for master's degrees at Aberystwyth by members of the team which prepared *The Social Accounts of the Welsh Economy*. As this book goes to press it was learnt that official estimates of gross domestic product in Northern Ireland were shortly to be published. It was impossible to take account of these estimates in the present study, but since they are constructed by similar methods, they should provide some interesting comparisons.

While this book was being published the official Scottish index of industrial production was revised with the result that manufacturing output is now shown to have expanded much more rapidly than was previously estimated. In particular, this revision has had the effect of tripling the rate of growth in this sector between the years 1954 and 1958. It was too late to take account of this in the text, but a number of footnotes have been added where relevant to indicate the significance of these changes and their full implications are discussed in a note on page 136.

I would like to thank Professor D. J. Robertson, Professor T. Wilson, Dr Laurence C. Hunter and Mr Malcolm MacLennan, all of whom read drafts of the book and made many helpful suggestions. I am particularly indebted to the Statistics Office of the Inland Revenue for providing information on Schedule E earnings in Scotland, which played an important part in the estimation of gross domestic product, and to the Scottish Statistics Office and the Economic Advisory Office of Northern Ireland for comments on Chapter 5. Finally I would like to thank Mrs Doris Ryder for her indispensable secretarial assistance.

University of Glasgow   GAVIN MCCRONE
February 27, 1964

CONTENTS

PREFACE	page	7
LIST OF TABLES		11
1 Introduction		13
2 Gross Domestic Product and Its Composition		20
3 Income from Employment, Gross Profits and Other Trading Income		37
4 The Output of Manufacturing Industry		47
5 The Prices of Manufacturing Output		57
6 Personal Income in the Standard Regions of the United Kingdom		66
7 Personal Income in the Main Regions and Counties of Scotland		81
8 Consumers' Expenditure in the Standard Regions		90
9 Investment in Scotland and Other Regions of the United Kingdom		99
10 Investment and Growth		106
11 Summary of the Main Findings and the Need for Further Improvement in Regional Statistics		119
12 The Implications for Policy		129
A Note on the Revision of the Index of Industrial Production		136
APPENDIX Sources and Methods		138
PART I: GROSS DOMESTIC PRODUCT AND THE OUTPUT OF MANUFACTURING INDUSTRY		
I Agriculture, Forestry and Fishing		140
II Manufacturing, Mining and Quarrying, Gas, Electricity and Water		143
III Construction		156
IV Transport and Communication		157
V Distributive Trades		162
VI Insurance, Banking and Finance		164
VII Other Services		166

VIII	Public Administration and Defence	167
IX	Public Health Services	168
X	Local Authority Educational Services	169
XI	Ownership of Dwellings	169
XII	Domestic Services to Households	170
XIII	Services to Private Non-Profit Making Bodies	170
XIV	Gross Domestic Product at Constant Prices	171
	PART II: INCOME FROM EMPLOYMENT, GROSS PROFITS AND OTHER TRADING INCOME	172
	PART III: INVESTMENT	176
	INDEX	178

LIST OF TABLES

	page
Gross Domestic Product 1951–60	31
Comparison of Gross Domestic Product with United Kingdom	32
Gross Domestic Product by Industry of Origin	33
Gross Domestic Product per head of Total Population by Sectors	34
Output per head of Occupied Population by Industries	34
Gross Domestic Product at 1954 Prices	35
Gross Domestic Product at 1954 Prices (Index)	36
Income from Employment 1951–60	42
Scottish Income from Employment Compared with United Kingdom	43
Income per Employee by Industries	44
Gross Profits: Income from Self-Employment and Other Trading Income	45
Gross Profits, Income from Self-Employment and Other Trading Income as a Proportion of G.D.P. by Industries	45
Income from Self-Employment, Gross Profits of Companies, etc.	46
Manufacturing Industry Net Output 1951–60	53
Percentage Distribution of Net Output	54
Growth of Manufacturing Output 1951–60	55
Output per Person Employed by Industries	56
Salaries as a Percentage of Employment Income	56
Prices of Net Output of Manufacturing Industry	59
Price Increases by Industries 1954–58	60
Personal Income by Regions 1959–60	77
Income per head of Total Population	78
Types of Income per head of Total Population	78
Relative Importance of Salaries, Property and Investment Income	79
Activity Rates and Unemployment by Regions (1959)	79
Income per Employee	80
Income per Person Assessed for Tax	80
Personal Income in the Main Regions of Scotland	88
Personal Income per Head of Total Population by Counties	89
Expenditure per Head 1953–54	96

	page	
Expenditure per Head 1961–62		97
Expenditure per Household 1961–62		98
Fixed Investment in Manufacturing Industry 1951–60		102
Fixed Investment at Constant Prices (Index)		102
Investment as a Percentage of Gross Domestic Product in Manufacturing 1951–60		103
Fixed Investment in Manufacturing by Industries		104
Other Capital Expenditure		105
Other Capital Expenditure as a Percentage of United Kingdom		105
Gross Investment, Growth and Gross Marginal Capital/Output Ratios		109
Net Investment, Growth and Net Marginal Capital/Output Ratios		112
Net Investment, Growth of Productivity and Net Marginal Investment/Productivity Ratios		116

CHAPTER 1

INTRODUCTION

IN recent years it has become increasingly clear that one of Britain's major economic problems is the lack of regional balance in the country's economic performance. It seemed that economic growth was increasingly centred on the Midlands and South-East of England, while some other parts of the country suffered rising unemployment and economic stagnation. Apart from the regional problem, however, Britain itself has had a poor rate of economic growth during the last decade. It may be argued that this is at least partly because the areas where there has been an impetus for growth have had relatively few spare resources, and inflation has therefore been a constant danger. Other regions which have had unemployed resources and a considerable growth potential have lacked the impetus. It may be, therefore, that a positive regional policy could also improve the country's overall economic position.

A substantial amount has been written on regional economic problems at a variety of levels. Most notable of recent studies have been the two reports on Scotland and Northern Ireland and the White Papers on Central Scotland and North-East England.[1] As a result the main issues of regional policy are now clear and a number of possible approaches to the problem have been canvassed. However, all the studies which have been made so far have been handicapped by a shortage of statistical material. This prevents the analysis of certain problems from being as complete as might be desired; for others it makes analysis impossible altogether. It is therefore scarcely surprising that in popular writings and in common discussion, analysis is frequently replaced by assertion.

[1] *Report of the Committee of Inquiry into the Scottish Economy*, Scottish Council (Development & Industry) 1961 (Toothill Committee). *Report of the Joint Working Party on the Economy of Northern Ireland*, H.M.S.O., London, Cmnd. 1835. *Central Scotland: A Programme for Development & Growth*, Cmnd. 2188, H.M.S.O., Edinburgh. November 1963. *The North-East: A Programme for Development & Growth*, Cmnd. 2206. H.M.S.O., London. November 1963.

The state of statistical information on the regions varies greatly from one region to another, though on none can it be said to be adequate. Northern Ireland is by far the best supplied, doubtless as a result of its particular system of administration and its geographical isolation. A fairly detailed Census of Production is available for each year, and figures for exports and imports, personal income, industrial production, capital investment and wages and salaries are regularly published.[1]

No such detail is available for Scotland, though the Digest of Scottish Statistics does give much information which is not available for other regions including an index of industrial production.[2] The Inland Revenue returns likewise provide more information on Scotland than for other regions, apart from Northern Ireland; and the United Kingdom Census of Production contains figures for Scotland and Wales which are not available for the regions of England.[3] Scotland also has the advantage, unlike Wales, of being a distinct region for many of the nationalized industries, so that separate figures are more readily obtained from their annual reports than for other areas.

The position for Wales is similar to Scotland, though not quite so good. The Digest of Welsh Statistics provides much useful information, but there is no index of industrial production.[4] For most purposes Wales is bracketed with England in the Inland Revenue reports; and the nationalized industries in defining the regions of their activities, tend to amalgamate parts of Wales with neighbouring counties of England.

These three regions are, however, in a far better position than any of the regions of England. For them the provision of statistical information is extremely poor and an analysis of their economic condition is therefore much more difficult. One has to rely chiefly on employment statistics and figures for earnings which have only recently been published, a certain amount of information in the Census of Production and the periodic income censuses published in the Inland Revenue reports.[5] It is perhaps partly because of the lack of information that the regions of England have had much less written

---

[1] *Digest of Statistics*, Government of Northern Ireland, H.M.S.O., Belfast. *Reports on the Census of Production of Northern Ireland*, H.M.S.O., Belfast.

[2] *Digest of Scottish Statistics*, Scottish Statistical Office, H.M.S.O., Edinburgh.

[3] *Reports of the Commissioners of Her Majesty's Inland Revenue* (Annual), H.M.S.O., London. *Census of Production*, Board of Trade, H.M.S.O., London.

[4] *Digest of Welsh Statistics*, H.M.S.O., London.

[5] *Statistics on Incomes, Prices, Employment and Production*, Ministry of Labour, H.M.S.O., London.

INTRODUCTION

about their economic problems than Northern Ireland, Scotland or Wales.

One of the main statistical gaps for all the regions is the absence of estimates corresponding to national income, gross national product or gross domestic product which might be compared with the *National Income and Expenditure* Accounts of the United Kingdom.[1] This would provide a way of measuring the relative levels of income and output in the different regions. Without it very little is known of their comparative efficiency or standards of living. If such estimates were produced regularly they could also provide useful information on the economic growth of regions, being much wider in coverage than the indices of industrial production which are at present available for Northern Ireland and Scotland. Furthermore, if the estimates were built up industry by industry they would provide an analysis of the economic structure of regions; and when set beside statistics for employment, they would give comparative figures of output per head in different industries.

The present study presents such estimates for Scotland over the period 1951–1960. Though writing in 1963 it was impossible to go beyond 1960 owing to the lack of published material (the latest Census of Production to be published was 1958). Previous studies in this field include Professor A. D. Campbell's estimates of Scottish national income over the period 1924–49. For Northern Ireland there are Mr N. Cuthbert's estimate of private civilian income 1935–6 to 1951–2 and Professor C. F. Carter and Mary Robson's national income and social accounts for Northern Ireland for 1952; this latter study was subsequently extended to provide estimates of gross domestic product in Northern Ireland covering the years 1950 to 1956. The Welsh studies comprise Professor E. T. Nevin's *Social Accounts of the Welsh Economy, 1948 to 1956*, and a separate estimate of gross domestic product in Wales for 1948 by Dr J. Parry Lewis.[2]

[1] *National Income and Expenditure*, Central Statistical Office, H.M.S.O., London.

[2] A. D. Campbell, 'Changes in Scottish Incomes, 1924–49', *Economic Journal*, 1955, and 'Income', chap. 5 in *The Scottish Economy*, edited by A. K. Cairncross, Cambridge, 1954; K. S. Isles and N. Cuthbert, *An Economic Survey of Northern Ireland*, H.M.S.O., Belfast, 1957, Appendix A; C. F. Carter and Mary Robson, A Comparison of the National Incomes and Social Accounts of Northern Ireland, the Republic of Ireland and the United Kingdom, *Journal of the Statistical and Social Inquiry Society of Ireland*, 108th Session 1954–5, pp. 62–87; and C. F. Carter, *Estimates of the Gross Domestic Product of Northern Ireland, 1950–56*, ibid., 112th Session, 1938–39, p. 149. E. T. Nevin (editor), *The Social Accounts of the Welsh Economy, 1948–56*, Welsh Economic Studies No. 2, University of

The estimates presented in this book have derived great benefit from these earlier studies; but in scope and form of presentation they differ in some important respects. Because the provision of basic statistical material for Scotland is not as good as for Northern Ireland, it is not possible to construct social accounts for Scotland in such detail as can be done for Northern Ireland without throwing caution to the winds and making a series of very hazardous assumptions. On the other hand it should be possible to present better estimates than for Wales.

In view of this it is perhaps surprising that the most detailed and comprehensive estimates so far published are Professor Nevin's *Social Accounts of the Welsh Economy*. These contain estimates of income and expenditure, investment in fixed capital formation and in stocks, current account of local authorities and the revenue account of central government. In fact they follow very closely the pattern of the United Kingdom *National Income and Expenditure*. They are only able to do this, however, by making a number of seemingly doubtful assumptions. Thus the estimates for capital formation, saving and expenditure, for instance, are very much less satisfactory than one would wish and may actually be misleading.

It may be that it is a mistake to try to follow too closely the framework of the United Kingdom national income accounts in presenting estimates for regions. One of the main purposes of making regional estimates is to draw comparisons with the United Kingdom as a whole; it is important therefore that the figures should properly reflect the regional disparities. Attempts to produce a full set of social accounts for regions are commonly forced to derive many of their estimates from some sort of ratio, such as the population ratio, applied to the national figure. Unless the ratio is a really appropriate one, this type of procedure is apt to destroy the whole purpose of the study. Such ratios may make the region appear to reflect the characteristics of the rest of the nation more closely than is actually the case, and so minimize the differences one is trying to discover. Furthermore, if a fair proportion of the estimates are founded on a rather shaky basis, this may also destroy confidence in the remainder.

In some respects therefore the estimates presented in this study are less ambitious in coverage than the Welsh figures contained in Professor Nevin's study. On the other hand much more attention is given

---

Wales Press, 1957; J. Parry Lewis, 'Income and Consumer's Expenditure', chap. 8 in *The Welsh Economy*, edited by Brinley Thomas, University of Wales Press, 1961.

INTRODUCTION

to comparisons with other regions and with the United Kingdom as a whole. Comparisons between Scotland and other regions have therefore been made wherever possible.

The estimates presented here are not sufficiently comprehensive to constitute a set of social accounts. In some respects it was tempting to try to produce one, but the available data were far from adequate. In the circumstances it seemed much better to limit the study to those estimates which could be presented with a good claim to accuracy.

Even so the methods which had to be used in deriving the estimates were often extremely complicated as a glance at the Appendix will show. It is particularly regrettable that so many Government statistics are not presented on a comparable basis covering a number of years. For example numerous adjustments had to be made to Census of Production figures to get a continuous series of estimates; and one way or another the change in the Standard Industrial Classification caused several months of additional work. Differences of definition between Government departments also tend to produce confusion. It is unfortunate, for example, that differences between the basis of Ministry of Labour figures and those of other departments frequently made certain estimates difficult to obtain and unreliable once they were obtained.

Previous studies have taken national income, gross national product or private civilian income as the cornerstone of their estimates. In this book, however, attention is primarily focused on gross domestic product and its composition rather than gross national product or national income. Gross domestic product may be regarded as measuring the income originating within the region rather than the income ultimately received within the region, which is gross national product. It happens that gross domestic product can be estimated with much more reliability for regions than gross national product, because of the lack of information on flows of property income either into or out of the region. But, apart from this, it is in many ways the more significant figure for studying the economy of a region. For a region it is possible to envisage a much wider divergence between gross domestic product and gross national product than is common for a nation, since a large part of the industrial plant of the region may be owned by outsiders and equally the property income of those within the region may derive in large part from property shares, etc. in other regions. It would thus be theoretically possible for gross domestic product to be falling at a time when gross national product of a region was rising. This is admittedly unlikely, but it seems clear that gross domestic product is the better measure of a region's economic performance. In this respect, therefore, the present estimates differ from those of Professor Campbell who was concerned with Scottish national income defined as income ultimately accruing to people in Scotland whether from within the region or outside.[1]

Another feature of the present study is that estimates of gross domestic product are obtained by the addition of estimates for individual industries. In this it follows the procedure adopted both by Professor Carter and Mary Robson and also by Professor Nevin.[2] This procedure has the advantage that it provides an analysis of the economic structure of the region, and a number of interesting comparisons may be made between Scotland, the United Kingdom, Wales and Northern Ireland. This method also makes possible the use of the Census of Production as a principal source rather than relying entirely on the Inland Revenue figures. These are thought to be less satisfactory as a source, since the region in which an establishment is located may differ from the one to which its income is accredited for tax purposes.

Chapters 6 and 7 analyse the distribution of personal income between regions of the United Kingdom and between counties within Scotland. In this case the basic source was the reports of the Inland Revenue and it seemed better to draw the comparisons direct from the Inland Revenue figures than to try to adjust the figures by a series of crude procedures to some sort of National Accounting definitions.

In Chapters 9 and 10 an analysis is made of investment in Scotland and in Wales and Northern Ireland. It was decided that complete figures for all Scottish investment could not be satisfactorily constructed not only for practical but also for conceptual reasons. Despite this a number of interesting comparisons can be made especially for investment in manufacturing industry. In Chapter 10 this is related to growth, and the productivity of investment in terms of growth is assessed for Scotland, Wales and Northern Ireland.

The Sources and Methods of the gross domestic product and other estimates are given at considerable length in the Appendix. This was done for two reasons. In the first place, many of the techniques and procedures used in this type of work are, of necessity, devious and complicated. It is therefore important that those using figures in this book should know precisely what degree of reliability to attach to them. This knowledge can only be obtained by referring to the de-

---

[1] A. D. Campbell, op. cit.
[2] Op. cit.

INTRODUCTION

tailed methods used in the construction of the estimates. Without this, there is a tendency either to derive conclusions from the estimates which are unwarranted, or to regard all the estimates as suspect because a few had to be based on rather shaky assumptions.

It is hoped that at some time estimates of this kind will be continued and improved not only for Scotland but also for other regions. A similar hope was expressed by Professor Carter and Mary Robson.[1] There is little doubt that a series of estimates produced regularly for the regions of the United Kingdom would do much to improve our understanding of regional economic problems. But it is important that anyone who undertakes such studies should take over the techniques of previous work and improve on it without having to negotiate all the difficulties and pitfalls afresh. It is believed that the publication of a comprehensive Sources and Methods with the present study would enable revised estimates for Scotland to be prepared from time to time with only a fraction of the work required for the original study.

[1] Op. cit., p. 62.

CHAPTER 2

GROSS DOMESTIC PRODUCT AND ITS COMPOSITION

SCOTTISH GROSS DOMESTIC PRODUCT COMPARED WITH THE U.K.

GROSS domestic product may be regarded as the output or value added of all branches of industry and services in Scotland; alternatively it comprises income from employment (including wages, salaries and employers national insurance and superannuation contributions), income from self employment, company profits (including provision for depreciation), trading surpluses of public corporations and rent. It was impossible to compile estimates for all sectors using the same method; some were therefore calculated by measuring output, others by estimating the components of income.[1] All the estimates presented include stock appreciation, since it was felt that no method of deducting this which might be tried could be really satisfactory. The estimates differ from gross national product in that they do not include net income from outside the region, and from national income in that the latter also excludes provision for depreciation.

The estimates of Scotland's gross domestic product are presented in Table I. This table also shows the composition of gross domestic product by the main industry and service groups. The two aspects of most immediate interest are the changes in Scottish gross domestic product over the period and the comparison of the Scottish estimates with the United Kingdom. Scottish gross domestic product rose from £1,238 million in 1951 to £1,964 million in 1960, an increase of 59 per cent. In the same period the equivalent rise for the United Kingdom was 70 per cent. A substantial part of this rise is accounted for by inflation in both cases, but it is nonetheless interesting to note that Scotland has been lagging behind the United Kingdom. Furthermore the indices for Scotland and the United Kingdom kept very close during the first three years; they began to diverge in 1954, but the divergence suddenly increased in 1959 and 1960 (see Table II).

The figures showing the percentage share of United Kingdom gross domestic product accounted for by Scotland give a similar picture. Scottish gross domestic product fell from 9·3 per cent of the

[1] See Appendix, 'Sources and Methods'.

GROSS DOMESTIC PRODUCT AND ITS COMPOSITION

United Kingdom total in 1951 to 8·7 per cent in 1960. The figure fluctuates slightly: after falling to 9·1 per cent in the years 1954–56 it recovers to 9·2 per cent in 1957 before falling once again. It is often asserted that Scotland experiences larger trade cycle fluctuations than the United Kingdom, suffering more severely in times of depression because of the nature of the industry. These figures perhaps may be said to give evidence of this. 1951 was a year of high boom and the Scottish figure was high. Thereafter follows a slight recession and stagnation in the middle fifties; 1956 and 1957 see a recovery and an improvement in the Scottish figure once again. 1958 brings a fairly sharp recession and an immediate fall in the Scottish figure. This is accentuated in 1959 and 1960 when the United Kingdom economy begins to recover; but on this occasion the recovery is much less marked in Scotland so that the lag is increased.

If gross domestic product is expressed per head of the population this gives some idea of the relative standard of living. It is not an exact measurement, because it excludes net income from other regions and abroad and it fails to take account of relative price levels. This latter is not really such a serious problem when comparing parts of one economy, where prices are generally fairly similar, as it is for international comparisons, say between France and the United Kingdom; but ideally it should be taken into account. It is commonly believed that the cost of living is higher in London than in the provinces of England, and it seems pretty certain that it is also high in the islands and parts of the highlands of Scotland. No figures are available, however, and it is therefore not possible to make appropriate adjustments.

The figures show that gross domestic product per head in Scotland fell from approximately 92 per cent of the United Kingdom figure in 1951 to 88 per cent in 1960. These figures fit in fairly well with Professor Campbell's earlier estimates of national income, which gave 93 per cent in 1949.[1] Any differences arising may well be accounted for by the difference in definition between Campbell's national income and gross domestic product used here. Once again there is evidence that Scotland is falling behind; but the Scottish figure is not far below the United Kingdom level, especially at the start of the period, and there may be those who would expect a wider gap.

On the evidence of comparisons made between the United Kingdom and other European countries, this means that Scotland has a standard of living equal to many in Europe and better than several. Studies of this type are notoriously difficult to make, and those who

[1] A. D. Campbell, op. cit.

attempt them invariably get slightly differing results. But the study by Milton Gilbert, which gave comparative figures for gross national product per head in eight European countries, shows that the majority of Western European countries were behind the United Kingdom level in 1955.[1] At that time probably the only exceptions were Switzerland and Sweden. Gilbert's figures expressed as a percentage of the United Kingdom gross national product per head were as follows: Norway 98, Belgium 96, Denmark 90, West Germany 86, France 84, Netherlands 82, and Italy 47.

In 1955 Scottish gross domestic product per head was 90 per cent of the United Kingdom level. Allowing for the inaccuracies which inevitably arise in such comparisons, it could probably be said that at this time the Scottish level was only exceeded by Norway and Belgium (among the countries in the study). The Danish level was probably very close to the Scottish, so also was the German. The remaining countries were perhaps somewhat behind. Today the picture has changed somewhat as a result of the rapid rate of economic growth in most of the Continental countries. Germany is now thought to have more or less caught up with the United Kingdom level and France is not far behind.[2] On the other hand the Scottish position since 1955 has tended to worsen in relation to the United Kingdom. It may be, therefore, that the Scottish level of gross domestic product per head is now only above that of the Netherlands and Italy.

But although Scotland, like the United Kingdom, has failed to keep up with the other countries, it is far from being a poor country. The comparison with Italy illustrates this. And Professor Carter's figures give the Irish Republic a level of gross national product per head which is only 51–52 per cent of the United Kingdom figure.[3] Scotland is in an entirely different category from these countries. Given a satisfactory rate of economic growth it could very soon catch up the other countries in the wealthy West European group.

Comparison with most of the standard regions of the United Kingdom is impossible except on the basis of personal income. (This comparison is made in a later chapter.) However, gross domestic product estimates are available for Northern Ireland and Wales. In 1956 Northern Ireland had a gross domestic product per head which was

[1] Milton Gilbert and Associates, *Comparative National Product, and Price Levels*, O.E.E.C., Paris, 1958.
[2] See for instance A. Lamfalussy, *The United Kingdom and the Six*, Macmillan, 1963, chap. 2, p. 19, where Gilbert's estimates are extended.
[3] C. F. Carter and Mary Robson, op. cit., p. 68.

66 per cent of the United Kingdom level.[1] The Welsh figure for the same year was 85 per cent.[2] Both these regions would therefore appear at this time to be worse off than Scotland. The difference between Scotland and Northern Ireland is clearly considerable; with Wales it is smaller and may by now have virtually disappeared.

Figures for gross domestic product per head of the working population give a somewhat different picture. If working population is taken as including unemployed, the Scottish product per head falls from approximately 95 per cent of the United Kingdom level in 1951 to 92 per cent in 1960 (Table II), a slightly smaller fall than gross domestic product per head of total population. Furthermore, if the unemployed are excluded, the gap between the Scottish and United Kingdom figures is reduced, and the fall is from 96 per cent to 94 per cent. Not only is the fall smaller, but in both of these cases the bulk of it takes place in the last two years.

These figures therefore show that part of the difference between Scottish gross domestic product per head of the total population and that of the United Kingdom is accounted for by a smaller working population in Scotland as a percentage of the total. This is especially so if unemployment is deducted, but applies even without this. This lower level of participation may be due to several factors.[3] Lack of opportunities may prevent married women and retired people from taking jobs to the extent that they do in the Midlands or the South-East. The slightly higher Scottish birth-rate tends to result in a higher proportion of children. And finally, lack of suitable employment forces many of the more enterprising Scots to seek work in the south. This results in high emigration; but in some cases it may be only the able-bodied members of the families who leave, many of the remainder staying in Scotland.[4]

It follows from this that if the Scottish working population could be expanded so that it formed the same proportion of total population as it does in the United Kingdom, Scottish gross domestic product per head might rise to 94 or 95 per cent of the United Kingdom level. There would still be a gap of some 5 or 6 per cent which is accounted for by a lower level of productivity per person employed in Scotland, but this is only about half of the present difference

[1] C. F. Carter, *Estimate of Gross Domestic Product of Northern Ireland, 1950–56*, op. cit., p. 149.

[2] E. T. Nevin (ed.), op. cit.

[3] The level of participation is discussed at greater length in Chapter 6, see Table V.

[4] Emigration was estimated at two hundred and fifty-five thousand between 1951 and 1961. (*Census of Population 1961.*)

between gross domestic product per head in Scotland and in the United Kingdom as a whole.

THE COMPOSITION OF GROSS DOMESTIC PRODUCT

The most interesting feature of the composition of Scotland's gross domestic product is its apparent similarity to that of the United Kingdom. This is illustrated in Table III. Admittedly the breakdown by broad industry groups may conceal disparities within groups: this is especially true of manufacturing industry which is further analysed in Chapter 4. But the similarity between Scotland and the United Kingdom is nonetheless surprising. For instance, the structure of the Scottish economy analysed in this way bears more resemblance to the United Kingdom than does that of Wales or Northern Ireland. Employment figures suggest that it is also closer to the United Kingdom than many of the English regions which tend to be more specialized. And it certainly bears more similarity to the United Kingdom economy than most other European countries, where agriculture plays a much larger part in the economy. This apparent structural similarity between the Scottish economy and the United Kingdom as a whole may be partly connected with size and location. Scotland is large enough for most of the major industries to be represented in some form, and its geographical separation may require a greater degree of self-reliance than is necessary for some of the English regions.

Table III shows that the industries with a larger share in the Scottish economy than in the United Kingdom are: agriculture, forestry and fishing, mining and quarrying, transport and communication, other services, public administration and defence, public health service and local authority education. But in most cases the difference is very slight, less than one percentage point. The main discrepancies are agriculture, forestry and fishing, which are 2·1 per cent higher in Scotland than in the United Kingdom, manufacturing which is 1·3 per cent lower, and distribution which is 1·4 per cent lower. The discrepancy in the first group arises mainly because Scotland has a large share of United Kingdom forestry and fishing. Indeed, Scotland has about a third of the total United Kingdom employment and about 24–29 per cent of the income from these two industries. Scottish agricultural output on the other hand was about 12 per cent of the United Kingdom total, only 2 per cent above the population proportion.[1]

[1] See Appendix, 'Sources and Methods', p. 140.

GROSS DOMESTIC PRODUCT AND ITS COMPOSITION

Comparison with Wales and Northern Ireland shows much wider differences. Agriculture, forestry and fishing accounts for 17·4 per cent of Northern Ireland's gross domestic product compared with 4·3 per cent for the United Kingdom. Mining and quarrying is of comparatively little importance in Northern Ireland and very important in Wales, where its share of gross domestic product is about three times that of the United Kingdom. Manufacturing plays a smaller part in both of these regions than it does in either Scotland or the United Kingdom, so does public administration and defence. Distribution plays a comparatively small part in Wales. On the other hand construction is more important in both areas.

In recent years comments on the Scottish economic situation have made much of Scotland's so-called structural disadvantage and it is surprising therefore to see how close the pattern of the Scottish economy is to that of the United Kingdom. Analysed in this way the structural disadvantage appears to be negligible; but this may be a false impression. Wide variations may occur in the types of industry within one industry group. Just as Northern Ireland has a much less efficient agriculture than the rest of the United Kingdom, so Scotland could be saddled with the less advanced sections of manufacturing industry.[1]

Since Scotland has a lower gross domestic product per head of total population than the United Kingdom as a whole, the figures in Table III do not give a clear picture of the share of a particular industry or service in Scotland in relation to the population. For example, it would be possible for a particular industry to account for a larger share of Scottish gross domestic product than in the United Kingdom, and yet output in relation to the Scottish population may be no greater than for the United Kingdom.

This question is analysed in Table IV where the contribution of each industry to gross domestic product is expressed per head of the total population. The Scottish figure is given as a percentage of the figure for the United Kingdom. Since 1958 was a year of depression, and possibly a depression which was more acute in Scotland than in the United Kingdom, comparative figures are also given for 1954. It will be seen that the Scottish output per head of total population exceeded that of the United Kingdom in agriculture, forestry and fishing by over 30 per cent in both years; it also exceeded the United Kingdom in local authority education and public health services. In 1954 it exceeded the United Kingdom figure in mining and quarrying, and in transport and communication, though the difference in

[1] This point is further discussed in Chapter 4.

the latter was very small. The industries where output per head of total population lagged furthest behind the United Kingdom were insurance, banking, and finance, distribution, ownership of dwellings and manufacturing.

Output per head of the occupied population in each industry is surprisingly difficult to calculate with accuracy owing to the difference between the definitions used by the Ministry of Labour in compiling figures of occupied population and those used for national income purposes. For example, many of those classified under manufacturing by the Ministry of Labour are grouped under transport and distribution in the national income estimates. Since it is impossible to make satisfactory adjustments for this, little significance can be attached to the actual figure of output per head in some industries.[1]

However, by using employment figures from the Census of Production, accurate figures can be obtained for manufacturing, gas, electricity and water, and mining and quarrying. And, if it is assumed that the difference in definition between the employment figures and the output figures affect Scotland and the United Kingdom in the same degree, then it is still possible to express Scottish output per head as a proportion of the United Kingdom with meaningful results.

The figures for a number of industries are given in Table V. It will be seen that, of the industries listed, Scottish output per head exceeds the United Kingdom only in gas, electricity and water. This presumably reflects the low employment ratio in hydro-electric production. Scottish output per head is very close to the United Kingdom in agriculture, forestry and fishing and in manufacturing. It is interesting that the figures for these industries should be so close to the United Kingdom level. It is sometimes thought that Scottish agriculture must be inefficient because of the crofting problem. But of course the crofting counties provide only a small share of Scottish agricultural output and the industry taken as a whole has an output per head which is virtually up to the United Kingdom level. The figures for manufacturing show that whatever structural disadvantages Scotland may have, these do not take the form of giving Scotland a very much lower output per head than the United Kingdom as a whole. Northern Ireland, on the other hand, has a very low output per head in manufacturing industry and this is partly associated with structure as is shown in Chapter 4.

The industries where productivity is poorest when compared with

[1] See Appendix, p. 162.

GROSS DOMESTIC PRODUCT AND ITS COMPOSITION

United Kingdom are mining and quarrying, distribution and construction. The figure for mining and quarrying reflects the low profitability of Scottish coal mines in 1958; and the figure for distribution may result from the employment situation in Scotland, the relative ease with which labour could be obtained and the lack of other opportunities to draw labour into more productive work. If this is the case distribution may be regarded as a sort of pool of concealed unemployment.

Taking gross domestic product as a whole per head of the occupied population, it will be seen that the figures for Wales and Scotland are very similar, approximately 5–6 per cent below the United Kingdom level. On the other hand the Northern Ireland gross domestic product per head of working population is only 78 per cent of the United Kingdom level. This low figure for Northern Ireland is accounted for mainly by manufacturing, agriculture and construction (Table V); in all of these industries productivity is well below the United Kingdom level.

GROSS DOMESTIC PRODUCT AT CONSTANT PRICES

The growth of the Scottish economy can only be assessed properly if gross domestic product is expressed at constant prices. Figures at current prices in Table I contain price increases from year to year as well as an element of growth. Furthermore, Scottish growth cannot properly be compared with the United Kingdom at current prices, since it cannot be assumed that inflation affects the value of Scottish output to precisely the same extent as it affects the United Kingdom's. Indeed, the evidence suggests that Scottish output in manufacturing industry suffers more inflation than that of the United Kingdom while the output of Northern Ireland suffers less.[1]

Gross domestic product at constant prices is difficult to calculate owing to the total absence of Scottish price indices. For some industries United Kingdom indices had to be used and for others the Scottish index of industrial production could be used. This is a volume index and ought therefore to give the same results as a value index at constant prices. The index was applied to 1954 output in value terms and the resulting figures for the other years were taken as equivalent to output at 1954 prices. This procedure is not as satisfactory as it ought to be since the index of industrial production is only

[1] See Chapter 5.

an indicator and possibly contains a certain amount of error.[1] However, it was the only method available apart from deflating Scottish output figures by United Kingdom price indices, which seemed likely to be even less satisfactory. For some industries this latter method had to be used, as there was no alternative. But in general United Kingdom price indices are only used for industries where Scottish price trends are unlikely to diverge much from the United Kingdom. Of the estimates made in this way, those for agriculture, forestry and fishing are perhaps the most likely to be subject to this type of inaccuracy. (A full account of the methods used is given in the Appendix.)

The indices in Table VII show that Scottish gross domestic product rose in step with the United Kingdom up to 1954, thereafter it began to lag slightly and after 1958 the lag becomes considerable. Total growth between 1954 and 1960 was only 9 per cent compared with 18 per cent for the United Kingdom. A significant point is that whereas Scottish gross domestic product in real terms actually declines in 1958 with the onset of the recession, the United Kingdom gross domestic product has the pace of its advance checked but nonetheless shows a slight rise.

Despite this, the United Kingdom growth rate was one of the lowest in Europe during this period, its 18 per cent between 1954 and 1960 comparing with 50 per cent for Germany, 42 per cent for Italy, 30 per cent for France, 37 per cent for E.E.C. and 30 per cent for all the countries of O.E.C.D.[2] In contrast to such rates the 9 per cent growth of the Scottish economy seems exceptionally inadequate. Only the Irish Republic with 4 per cent growth put up a poorer performance than Scotland, and it has done very much better in more recent years.[3]

The chief reason for the slow growth of the Scottish economy is the lack of sufficient expansion in manufacturing industry, whose output likewise increased only 9 per cent in the period 1954 to 1960

---

[1] This is further discussed in Chapter 5. It should be emphasized that the figures used in this section rest heavily on the official Scottish indices of industrial production (*Digest of Scottish Statistics*). This is used as the basis for manufacturing, mining and quarrying, construction and gas, electricity and water. Since this was written the index has been revised to give higher rates of growth. Manufacturing output is now estimated at 106 per cent of the 1954 level in 1958 and approximately 114 per cent in 1960. The effect of this is to raise Gross Domestic Product at constant prices to 105 per cent of the 1954 level in 1958 and about 110 per cent in 1960 (see note on the revised index, p. 136).

[2] O.E.C.D. General Statistics.

[3] Ibid. Irish economic growth improved sharply towards the end of the 1950s.

GROSS DOMESTIC PRODUCT AND ITS COMPOSITION

compared with a 23 per cent rise in United Kingdom manufacturing output. But other industries also lagged; comparing the Scottish figures with those for the United Kingdom in Table VII, there is not an industry or service group, with the sole exception of rent from the ownership of dwellings, whose output in 1960 had not either risen more slowly or fallen more quickly than that of the United Kingdom. In agriculture, forestry and fishing the Scottish share of United Kingdom output fell in 1959 and 1960.[1] In mining and quarrying the decline of output was more rapid in Scotland than the rest of the United Kingdom, presumably because Scotland had a higher proportion of uneconomic pits which were being closed. Scotland's poor performance in manufacturing is perhaps not simply a failure of new growth to take place; but the new growth which has occurred has been insufficient to counteract the decline in traditional industries and also maintain a satisfactory overall rate of growth. Perhaps if there had not been a decline in such industries as shipbuilding and all the trades associated with it, Scotland's rate of growth might have come nearer to the United Kingdom level. But it is difficult to assess the extent of the decline which had to be counteracted or to estimate the amount of new growth taking place, since the statistics only show the net effect of these changes.

The tendency for other industries and services to lag is largely bound up with the three groups discussed above. In some degree or other their output may be tied to the prosperity of manufacturing, mining and quarrying and agriculture, forestry and fishing. Construction is certainly influenced to a great degree by housebuilding which, if it is publicly controlled, may not be greatly affected by economic conditions; but the rate of private housebuilding is associated with the prosperity of the regional economy and the industry's output also depends on factory construction. Similar factors tend to influence all the other groups in Tables VI and VII except public administration and defence which is governed by entirely different circumstances. The fact that the Scottish decline in this group was also more rapid than in the United Kingdom would seem to be associated with the ending of national service and may be largely fortuitous.

The lag of Scottish rates of growth behind the United Kingdom is obviously much accentuated in the last three years of the period. Comparing the Scottish 1957 figures with those for the United

[1] See Appendix, 'Sources and Methods', where a breakdown is given. The Scottish share of the U.K. total declined both in agriculture and forestry and fishing.

Kingdom in Table VII it would seem that Scotland was only slightly behind the United Kingdom at that time. The difference in rates of growth in agriculture, forestry and fishing, gas, electricity and water, and distribution was very small; in transport and communication, insurance, banking and finance and miscellaneous other services the rates were the same; and in construction, public administration and defence and ownership of dwellings, the Scottish rate was actually higher than the United Kingdom rate. Manufacturing, however, even in 1957 was showing quite a marked tendency to fall behind the United Kingdom growth rate, and mining and quarrying was already declining faster.

By contrast the earlier period, 1951–54, shows much less divergence between Scottish and United Kingdom growth rates. The overall rate of growth of gross domestic product is the same for both areas as also is the growth in manufacturing output. The Scottish rate is faster than the United Kingdom rate in construction, gas, electricity and water, distribution, public administration and ownership of dwellings, though the difference is often scarcely significant. The Scottish rate is slower in agriculture, forestry and fishing, transport and communication, insurance, banking and finance, and other services. Mining and quarrying shows a decline in Scotland and a slight expansion in the United Kingdom.

Thus the pattern which emerges is that growth of the Scottish economy keeps more or less in step with the United Kingdom from 1951–54. For 1954 to 1957 it begins to lag slightly, especially in manufacturing; and from 1957 to 1960 the lag becomes serious and emerges in all industries and service groups.

TABLE I
SCOTLAND
Gross Domestic Product   £ million

	1951	1952	1953	1954	1955	1956	1957	1958	1959	1960
Agriculture, Forestry & Fishing	97	107	105	103	99	110	112	113	109	113
Mining & Quarrying	50	56	59	59	62	70	72	68	65	62
Manufacturing	437	439	472	510	560	585	628	639	656	708
Construction	64	71	79	84	89	100	97	104	108	125
Gas, Electricity & Water	23	25	29	32	36	41	43	44	47	49
Transport & Communications	121	123	117	130	140	151	173	152	158	181
Distribution	152	145	153	169	182	191	204	195	209	219
Insurance, Banking & Finance	27	25	27	30	32	32	35	37	40	44
Other Services	106	108	110	109	127	131	140	148	155	160
Public Administration & Defence	76	83	88	92	95	105	110	117	118	122
Public Health Service	20	21	25	27	29	32	33	36	40	46
Local Authority Education	25	27	29	31	33	37	41	44	48	52
Ownership of Dwellings: Rent	25	28	32	37	39	43	48	55	61	64
Domestic Services	9	9	9	9	9	8	8	8	8	7
Services to Private Non-Profit making Bodies	6	7	7	7	7	8	9	10	11	12
G.D.P.*	1,238	1,274	1,341	1,429	1,539	1,644	1,753	1,770	1,833	1,964
G.D.P.* U.K.	13,287	13,694	14,510	15,638	16,964	18,157	19,116	19,709	20,893	22,560

* Excluding any allowance for stock appreciation.

Sources and Methods: See Appendix.

TABLE II
Comparison of Gross Domestic Product with U.K.

	1951	1952	1953	1954	1955	1956	1957	1958	1959	1960
SCOTTISH G.D.P. as % of U.K.	9·3	9·3	9·2	9·1	9·1	9·1	9·2	9·0	8·8	8·7
GDP. *per Head:* £										
SCOTLAND	243	249	262	279	300	320	340	342	353	377
U.K.	265	271	287	308	333	355	372	381	402	431
Scotland as % of U.K.	91·8	91·8	91·3	90·6	90·1	90·1	91·6	89·8	87·8	87·5
G.D.P. *per Head of Working Population:* £										
SCOTLAND	530	546	571	602	645	688	735	752	780	834
U.K.	558	574	606	645	693	736	772	800	845	902
Scotland as % of U.K.	94·9	95·1	94·3	93·3	93·1	93·6	95·2	94·0	92·3	92·5
G.D.P. *per Head of Working Population less Unemployed:* £										
SCOTLAND	542	561	586	617	658	702	752	776	811	861
U.K.	563	585	614	652	699	743	781	816	861	914
Scotland as % of U.K.	96·2	95·8	95·5	94·6	94·1	94·5	96·3	95·2	94·2	94·2
Scottish G.D.P. Index current prices	100	103	108	116	124	133	142	143	148	159
U.K. G.D.P. Index current prices	100	103	109	118	128	137	144	148	157	170

GROSS DOMESTIC PRODUCT AND ITS COMPOSITION

TABLE III

Gross Domestic Product by Industry of Origin

Percentage Distribution

	U.K.*	SCOTLAND	WALES	NORTHERN IRELAND
	1958	1958	1956	1956
Agriculture, Forestry and Fishing	4·3	6·4	5·5	17·4
Mining and Quarrying	3·6	3·8	11·3	·4
Manufacturing	37·4	36·1	32·1	32·1
Construction	5·9	5·9	7·0	6·2
Gas, Electricity and Water	2·7	2·5	2·9	2·0
Transport and Com.	8·2	8·6	7·9	6·1
Distribution	12·4	11·0	8·9	12·8
Insurance, Banking & Finance	2·9	2·1	2·0	2·1
Other Services	8·3	8·4	8·5	8·1
Public Administration and Defence	6·2	6·6	5·3	5·0
Public Health Services	1·7	2·0	4·3	2·2
Local Authority Educ.	2·0	2·5		2·3
Rent from Ownership of Dwellings	3·5	3·1	3·2	2·3
Domestic Service and Services to non-profit making bodies	1·0	1·0	1·0	1·0

* *Note:* United Kingdom figures for 1958 have been adjusted to definitions used prior to the change in standard industrial classification. The percentages given here therefore do not correspond exactly with the figures given for 1958 in *National Income and Expenditure*.

TABLE IV

SCOTLAND

G.D.P. per Head of Total Population by Sectors

U.K. = 100

	1954	1958
Agriculture, forestry and fishing..	134	132
Mining and Quarrying	104	96
Manufacturing	85	87
Construction	92	89
Gas, electricity and water	86	84
Transport and Com.	102	94
Distribution	86	80
Insurance, Banking and Finance	65	64
Other Services	84	91
Public Administration and Defence	93	95
Public Health Services	107	108
Local Authority Education	120	115
Rent from ownership of dwellings	69	75

Note: The Scottish population was 10·1 per cent of the U.K. total in 1954 and 10·0 per cent in 1958.

TABLE V

Output per Head of Occupied Population by Industries (1958)

As a percentage of U.K.

	SCOTLAND	WALES	NORTHERN IRELAND
Agriculture, forestry and fishing..	99	—	65†
Mining and Quarrying*	79·9	89·1	—
Manufacturing*	96·5	118·3	67·8
Construction	86	—	77·3*
Gas, Electricity and Water*	104·9	89·6	84·6
Transport and Com.	90	—	80·3‡
Distribution	82	—	87·4‡
Insurance, Banking and Finance..	90	—	—
Total G.D.P.	94·0	94·8‡	77·7‡

* Derived wholly from Census of Production figures.

† Agriculture only: from Digest of Statistics, Government of Northern Ireland, H.M.S.O., Belfast.

‡ Based on 1956. Figures taken from C. F. Carter, *Estimates of the Gross Domestic Product of Northern Ireland, 1950–56.* Journal of the Statistical and Social Inquiry Society of Ireland, 112th Section, 1958–59, p. 149. Welsh total from E. T. Nevin, op. cit.

TABLE VI

Gross Domestic Product at 1954 Prices £million

	1951	1952	1953	1954	1955	1956	1957	1958	1959	1960
Agriculture, Forestry & Fishing	98	105	103	103	97	109	109	106	105	109
Mining & Quarrying	61	60	60	59	58	57	57	53	51	48
Manufacturing	469	454	479	510	520	530	530	520	525	556
Construction	68	72	81	84	87	90	92	87	96	97
Gas, Electricity & Water	27	29	29	32	34	34	36	37	37	39
Transport & Communications	127	125	121	130	129	129	135	125	127	134
Distribution	152	149	157	169	174	174	181	172	183	183
Insurance, Banking & Finance	28	27	28	30	31	29	32	33	36	36
Public Administration & Defence	89	90	93	92	90	89	87	86	82	79
Rent from ownership of dwellings	33	35	36	37	38	39	41	39	41	42
All other services	179	179	183	183	190	194	205	218	223	229
G.D.P.	1,331	1,325	1,370	1,429	1,448	1,474	1,505	1,476	1,506	1,552

Note: The figures for manufacturing in this table are affected by the revision of the index of industrial production. As an example the revised estimate for 1958 would be £540 million and for 1960 about £580 million. This would raise GDP to £1,496 million and £1,592 million. See 'A Note on the Revision of the Index of Industrial Production', p. 136.

TABLE VII
SCOTLAND
Gross Domestic Product at 1954 Prices (Index)

	1951	1952	1953	1954	1955	1956	1957	1958	1959	1960	United Kingdom 1954=100		
											1951	1957	1960
Agriculture, Forestry & Fishing	96	102	100	100	94	106	106	103	102	106	94	107	114
Mining & Quarrying*	104	102	101	100	99	97	96	89	86	82	98	99	89
Manufacturing*	92	89	94	100	102	104	104	102	103	109	92	108	123
Construction*	81	86	96	100	104	107	110	104	114	116	87	106	118
Gas, Electricity & Water*	84	90	92	100	105	107	111	114	115	121	85	114	133
Transport & Communications	98	96	93	100	99	99	104	96	98	103	92	104	112
Distribution	90	88	93	100	103	103	107	102	108	108	91	108	121
Insurance, Banking & Finance	95	91	94	100	103	97	106	109	121	121	91	106	134
Public Administration & Defence	97	98	101	100	98	97	95	93	89	86	98	94	88
Rent from ownership of dwellings	90	94	96	100	102	106	112	106	112	113	97	106	110
All other services	98	98	100	100	104	106	112	119	122	125	93	112	130
G.D.P.	93	93	96	100	101	103	105	103	105	109			
G.D.P.:U.K.	93	92	96	100	104	105	106	107	112	118			

* Based on Scottish index of Industrial production.

Others based on U.K. price adjustments to Scottish estimates as calculated from B.B.

Note: The revised index gives higher figures for manufacturing after 1954. For example 1958 is 106 on the new basis and 1960 about 114. This raises GDP to 105 for 1958 and 110 for 1960 (see p. 136).

CHAPTER 3

INCOME FROM EMPLOYMENT, GROSS PROFITS & OTHER TRADING INCOME

ESTIMATES of Scottish income from employment are presented in Tables I and II. The estimates include wages and salaries and employers' contributions to superannuation and national insurance. It was not found possible to separate these components, except for a few industries in certain years, without making a series of assumptions more heroic than seemed justified.

The general pattern of income from employment shown in Tables I and II is similar to that which emerged for gross domestic product. The index in Table II shows that Scottish income rose less rapidly than that of the United Kingdom, though the difference in rate of growth is small at first and becomes much more marked after 1958. Perhaps most significant is the slow growth of income from employment in manufacturing in 1958 and 1959. The 1958 figure, indeed, is virtually the same as the 1957 figure. If allowance is made for inflation, this reflects the shrinkage in the labour force as a result of the recession.

As a proportion of the United Kingdom income from employment, the Scottish figure falls throughout the period from 9·3 per cent in 1951 to 8·6 per cent in 1960. The bulk of this fall, however, occurs in the last three years, illustrating once again that the recession starting in 1958 hit Scotland much more severely than the United Kingdom as a whole.

Scottish income per employee shows a similar trend, though the change is less marked. Income per employee starts the period at 94·6 per cent of the United Kingdom figure and remains approximately at this level until the last two years when it falls slightly. This presumably illustrates that employees' income in the region tends to keep in step with developments at the national level and is not influenced solely by the conditions of the regional economy.

Table III gives figures for income per employee by industries. This ought to provide an interesting comparison with the United Kingdom. But unfortunately it is extremely difficult to derive figures which are completely reliable; and the comparison is therefore not as satisfactory as one would wish. The main reason for the difficulty is the same as arose in Chapter 2 over estimates of gross domestic product per head of occupied population by industries.[1] The definitions used for national income accounts and those used by the Ministry of Labour for the published employment statistics differ considerably, so that straightforward division of income from employment figures by the numbers employed (less unemployed) according to the Ministry of Labour will not give a true figure for income per head by industries. This does not affect the figure for all industries combined; it is the allocation between industries which gives the trouble. The figures in Table III are therefore produced on the assumption that any error in the figures for income per head which arises in this way affects the United Kingdom and Scotland equally, so that the ratio of Scottish to United Kingdom income per head is not affected. This assumption seemed to be borne out by comparing the ratio thus obtained for manufacturing with figures derived entirely from the Census of Production. The difference was negligible.

The Scottish ratios for 1954 and 1958 are fairly similar.[2] Scottish income per employee falls behind the United Kingdom most in agriculture, forestry and fishing, construction and distribution. The first is slightly surprising since Scottish gross product per head in agriculture, forestry and fishing was so close to the United Kingdom level. But this was caused to a great extent by fishing. Taking income per employee in agriculture and horticulture alone, the Scottish figure comes to 92 per cent of the United Kingdom level. On the other hand, fishing in Scotland seemed to be typified by a remarkably high level of gross profits and a comparatively low level of regular employment income.[3]

The low level of income per employee in construction is less easy to explain, but it may be connected either with the pattern of work undertaken by the Scottish construction industry or the structure of the building firms. In distribution the availability of labour and the absence of other more profitable work to attract labour away may offer an explanation.

The industries where income per employee is higher in Scotland

[1] See Chapter 2, p. 26.

[2] The Scottish figures for 1954 may be subject to some slight error in the industry breakdown owing to the change made in the Scottish employment figure after 1955. (See footnote to Table III, also Appendix, p. 165.)

[3] See 'Sources and Methods', p. 141. This indicates that profit sharing and income from self-employment are more important in Scotland than in the United Kingdom as a whole where employees rely more on regular wages and salaries.

EMPLOYMENT, GROSS PROFITS AND TRADING INCOME

than in the United Kingdom are other services, public administration and defence, and in 1954 only, gas, electricity and water. Other services include the professional services and the higher figure may perhaps be connected either with the salary rates for Scottish teachers or the proportion of teachers with certain qualifications. The figure for public administration and defence is explained by a higher proportion of the total Scottish employment being in the armed forces. The United Kingdom figures show that pay in cash or kind of the armed forces comes out on average higher per head than employment income of civilian civil servants.[1]

The Welsh and Irish figures should provide some interesting comparisons with Scotland. But unfortunately for Northern Ireland one has to rely entirely on the Census of Production, and only three industries can be calculated. The results are much as might be expected: Northern Irish manufacturing industry gives a low income per employee mainly for structural reasons. Low paying industries such as textiles are heavily represented. The Welsh figures are much more surprising and in some instances scarcely credible. The high earnings in manufacturing result from the structure of Welsh manufacturing industry, in particular the large part played by metal manufacture. The figure for public administration and defence may be reasonable owing to the comparatively small proportion of civilian civil servants and the high proportion of armed forces. The high figures in construction and agriculture, forestry and fishing are less easy to understand. Construction may perhaps be influenced by the large amount of investment taking place in the Welsh economy and the consequent building of factories, etc.; but the figure for agriculture, forestry and fishing is quite bewildering.[2] Admittedly fishing plays a comparatively small part and employees are probably a smaller proportion of the agricultural population than in England, but it is hard to see how these features offer an explanation.

GROSS PROFITS AND OTHER TRADING INCOME

Following the definitions used in the United Kingdom *National Income and Expenditure*, this category includes the profits of companies and surpluses of public corporations before providing for depreciation; it also includes income from self-employment and rent. The figures are not quite so satisfactory as those for gross domestic

---

[1] In 1958 the former came to £765 and the latter to £567. Derived from the figures in *National Income and Expenditure, 1962* (Table 16).
[2] Investment in the Welsh economy is discussed in Chapter 8.

product and income from employment. This is partly because the figures for some industries are obtained by subtracting income from employment from gross product: a small percentage error in gross product could therefore become proportionately much larger in relation to gross profits. For other industries estimates had to be based on Schedule D Inland Revenue figures, and, as explained in the Appendix, if there is a discrepancy between region of assessment and of operation this could produce error.[1]

Table IV shows that the index of Scottish gross trading profits and other income follows a similar pattern to other Scottish indices. As with gross domestic product and income from employment, the Scottish rate of growth is less rapid than for the United Kingdom especially from 1958 onwards. The failure of profits to grow in 1958 as a result of the depression is more marked for Scotland than for the rest of the United Kingdom, the former declining while the latter has a 2 per cent rise. This is perhaps not unexpected since Scottish gross domestic product at constant prices also declined in 1958.

What is more surprising is that gross profits, etc. form the same proportion of gross domestic product in Scotland as they do in the United Kingdom both in 1954 and 1958 (see Table V). Yet the figures are far from identical if they are broken down by industries. Table V shows that in Scotland gross profits and other trading income form a higher proportion of gross product in agriculture, forestry and fishing, construction and transport and communication than they do in the United Kingdom. These figures are largely the obverse of the low levels found for income from employment in these same industries in Scotland. Fishing is again primarily responsible for the importance of profits in agriculture, forestry and fishing, and the type and size pattern of firms, no doubt accounts for much of the remainder. The extraordinarily low percentage of gross product accounted for by profits in mining and quarrying compared with the United Kingdom reflects the unprofitability of the Scottish coal industry. The high share accounted for by profits in gas, electricity and water is presumably caused by the importance of hydro-electricity in Scotland. The capital costs of hydro-electricity are high and there is presumably therefore a high depreciation charge which is included in these figures in accordance with the normal national income definitions.

The figures give Wales a very low level of gross profits in mining and quarrying; there is a low level also in construction and a high level in other services. These results are rather surprising and seem

[1] 'Sources and Methods', Appendix, p. 140, and under the industries concerned.

to be associated with the remarkably high level of income from employment in construction and the low level for other services (see Table II).

An interesting feature of the Scottish economy is the importance of income from self-employment. This forms a comparatively high proportion of the United Kingdom total (see Table VI). Sole traders and partnerships seem to be relatively more important in Scotland, possibly because firms have a different size structure or because the nature of the industry is slightly different. As a result people who might otherwise be salaried officials and included in income from employment receive a share in profits, and may be classified as self-employed. Table VI shows that Scottish income from self-employment is over 10 per cent of the United Kingdom total for most of the period.

If income from self-employment is deducted from the total for gross profits and other trading income, one is left with gross profits of companies, surpluses of public authorities and rent. Compared with United Kingdom figures it will be seen that this item has fallen as a proportion of the British total and its rate of growth, like all the other Scottish indices, is not so fast. An interesting feature is the comparative stagnation of Scottish profits in the earlier years and a sudden burst of growth in 1957. But in 1958 Scottish profits declined while United Kingdom profits continued to rise.

All these figures include imputed gross trading profits for those branches of companies operating in Scotland, but having their headquarters in other regions.[1] The gross profits of 'Scottish' companies in the sense that their headquarters are in Scotland may be roughly estimated from the Inland Revenue figures which correspond more approximately to this definition. It was found that on this basis 'Scottish' companies accounted for only 6–7 per cent of United Kingdom gross trading profits (see Table VI) and the share declined sharply in 1958. This gives some evidence of the degree to which Scotland is dependent on 'non Scottish' firms for the prosperity of the economy.

[1] The regional figures in the Census of Production reports are calculated on this basis.

TABLE I
SCOTLAND
Income from Employment (£ million)

	1951	1952	1953	1954	1955	1956	1957	1958	1959	1960
Agriculture, Forestry and Fishing	35	36	38	38	40	42	43	43	44	46
Mining & Quarrying	47	55	57	59	63	70	76	72	67	63
Manufacturing	272	297	321	338	369	403	424	425	438	469
Construction	50	56	61	66	71	79	79	83	85	99
Gas, Electricity & Water	12	13	14	15	17	18	20	20	22	23
Transport & Comm'cation	77	78	84	89	96	108	113	111	112	121
Distribution	77	79	83	89	96	104	113	116	123	122
Insurance, Banking & Finance	18	18	19	20	22	22	25	26	27	29
Other Services	66	66	68	66	80	86	92	97	98	98
Public Administration & Defence	76	83	88	92	95	105	110	117	118	122
Public Health Services	20	21	25	27	29	32	33	36	40	46
Loc. Authority Education	25	27	29	31	33	37	41	44	48	52
Domestic Service	9	9	9	9	9	8	8	8	8	7
Services to non-profit making bodies	6	7	7	7	7	8	9	10	11	12
Total	790	845	903	946	1,027	1,122	1,187	1,208	1,241	1,309

TABLE II

Scottish Income from Employment Compared with the U.K.

	1951	1952	1953	1954	1955	1956	1957	1958	1959	1960
Index 1951=100 Scotland	100	107	114	120	130	142	150	153	157	166
Index 1951=100 United Kingdom	100	108	114	121	132	144	153	159	166	178
As % of U.K.	9.3	9.3	9.4	9.2	9.2	9.2	9.2	9.0	8.8	8.6
Income per employee Scotland* £	382	412	437	452	488	530	562	584	604	630
Income per employee U.K.* £	404	438	457	480	517	558	586	615	641	674
Scot. Inc. per employee as % of U.K.*	94.6	94.1	95.6	94.2	94.4	94.9	95.9	94.6	94.2	93.5
Scot. Inc. per employee Index	100	108	114	118	128	139	147	153	158	165
U.K. Inc. per employee Index	100	108	113	119	128	138	145	152	159	167

* Insured Employees less unemployed. Scottish figures 1951–54 are adjusted for the addition of 12–13 thousand employees in accordance with the definition used since 1955.

TABLE III

Income per Employee by Industries*

U.K. = 100

	SCOTLAND 1954†	SCOTLAND 1958	WALES 1954[1]	N. IRELAND 1958[2]
Agriculture, Forestry & Fishing	84	82	122	—
Mining & Quarrying	100	100	95	—
Manufacturing	98	96	104[3]	75
Construction	79	82	136[4]	82
Gas, Electricity & Water	102	100	100	85
Transport & Communications	91	88	93	—
Distribution	82	83	98	—
Insurance, Banking & Finance	80	80	94	—
Public Administration & Defence	103	103	124	—
All other services	102	112	83	—
	94	95	105	

[1] Based on E. T. Nevin, *Social Accounts of the Welsh Economy, No. 2*, and *Digest of Welsh Statistics*.

[2] Census of Production.

[3] Based on Census of Production. Using Nevin's figures Welsh estimate comes to 111%.

[4] Comparison based on *National Income and Expenditure 1955* for U.K. The 1958 edition would bring the Welsh figure to 149.

Note:

* Insured employees less unemployed.

† See footnote to Table II. The appropriate adjustments have been made to total income per employee and to insurance, banking and finance which accounted for approximately 6,000 of the additional employees, but adjustments to other industries were impossible to make. Some of the 1954 figures in Table III may therefore be slightly too high.

EMPLOYMENT, GROSS PROFITS AND TRADING INCOME

TABLE IV
SCOTLAND
Gross Profits, Income from Self-Employment and Other Trading Income (£ million)

	1951	1952	1953	1954	1955	1956	1957	1958	1959	1960
Agriculture, forestry & fishing	62	71	67	65	59	68	69	70	65	67
Mining & Quarrying	3	1	2	0	−1	0	−4	−4	−2	−1
Manufact'ing	165	142	151	172	191	182	204	214	218	239
Construction	14	15	18	18	18	21	18	21	23	26
Gas, Electricity & Water	11	12	15	17	19	23	23	24	25	26
Transport & Comm.	44	45	33	41	44	43	60	41	46	60
Distribution	75	66	70	80	86	87	90	79	86	97
Insurance, Banking & Finance	9	7	8	10	10	10	10	11	13	15
Other Services	40	42	42	43	47	45	48	51	57	62
Ownership of Dwellings	25	28	32	37	39	43	48	55	61	64
	448	429	438	483	512	522	566	562	592	655
Scottish Index 1951=100	100	96	98	108	114	117	126	125	132	146
U.K.	100	95	102	111	119	124	130	132	142	156
Scotland as % of U.K.	9·3	9·4	9·0	9·0	9·0	8·8	9·1	8·9	8·7	8·8

TABLE V

Gross Profits, Income from Self-Employment and Other Trading Incomes as a Proportion of G.D.P. by Industries
(U.K.=100)

	SCOTLAND 1954	SCOTLAND 1958	WALES 1954
Agriculture, forestry and fishing	105	105	105
Mining and Quarrying	—	—	8
Manufacturing	97	106	103
Construction	105	95	60
Gas, Electricity and Water	116	109	96
Transport and Communication	114	104	89
Distribution	98	95	85
Other Services	97	83	180
Total	100	100	98

TABLE VI
SCOTLAND
Income from Self-Employment, Gross Profits of Companies, etc.

	1951	1952	1953	1954	1955	1956	1957	1958	1959	1960
					£ million					
Income from self-employment	153	161	163	165	170	178	179	182	187	197
Gross Profits of Companies, Surpluses, Rent	295	268	275	318	342	344	387	380	405	458
					Indices					
Income from self-employment Index	100	105	107	108	111	116	117	119	122	129
Gross Profits of Companies, etc. Index	100	91	93	108	116	117	131	129	137	155
Gross Profits of Companies, etc., Index United Kingdom	100	91	99	112	121	126	133	135	149	165
					Percentages					
Income from self-employment as % of U.K.	10·5	10·7	10·5	10·3	10·1	10·3	10·3	10·1	9·8	[9·8]*
Gross Profits of Companies, etc., as % of U.K.	8·8	8·8	8·3	8·5	8·4	8·2	8·8	8·4	8·1	[8·3]
Gross Profits of 'Scottish' Companies & Local Authorities as % of U.K.	6·6	6·7	6·3	6·7	6·3	7·1	6·5	5·8	6·1	—

* Obtained by guesswork since the Inland Revenue figures for 1960 were not available for self-employment income. The other estimates for 1960 are mostly dependent on this. (See Appendix.)

CHAPTER 4

THE OUTPUT OF MANUFACTURING INDUSTRY

THE output of manufacturing industry is the largest component part of gross domestic product, amounting to approximately 36 per cent of the Scottish total in 1958. But its importance is even greater than this percentage would indicate, since many other sectors of the economy are dependent in some degree on activity generated by manufacturing. Thus, distribution, banking, transport, and construction will all tend to expand if manufacturing expands; and equally they will be more likely to remain stagnant if manufacturing output fails to grow. A satisfactory rate of growth for manufacturing output is therefore of primary importance for the prosperity of the economy.

MANUFACTURING OUTPUT AND ITS COMPOSITION

The figures for Scottish manufacturing output at current prices are given by the main industrial orders in Table I. The distribution of types of manufacturing industry can be of great importance to the economy, since some types of manufacturing industry tend to enjoy more rapid growth than others and some are associated with higher output per head than others. Thus a poor rate of growth in the economy could result from a heavy representation of slow growing or declining industries; and low productivity could be the result of an abnormally high proportion of total output originating in industries with a low output per head.

It is commonly thought that Scotland suffers from the first of these, an economic structure which is heavily weighted by slow growing or declining industries. It is interesting, therefore, to compare the composition of Scottish manufacturing output by order groups with the United Kingdom and other regions of the British economy (see Table II). In fact, the pattern of Scottish output is much closer to that of the United Kingdom than is that of Wales or Northern Ireland. Indeed the apparent similarity of the composition of Scottish output and that of the United Kingdom is quite striking. Food, drink, and tobacco, metal manufacture, shipbuilding and marine engineering, textiles, and paper, printing and publishing are more heavily represented in Scotland than in the United Kingdom; this is especially so of food, drink and tobacco and shipbuilding, where the difference is considerable. The other industries play a slightly smaller part in the Scottish economy than they do in the rest of the United Kingdom. In most cases the difference is small, but it is substantial in vehicles and chemicals.

In contrast to this, the Welsh output is very heavily weighted by metal manufacture, which accounts for about 40 per cent of the total; chemicals also play a larger part than in the United Kingdom, but other industries tend to be under-represented, especially shipbuilding, vehicles, food, drink and tobacco, paper and printing, clothing and furniture. The composition of Northern Ireland output differs equally strikingly from that of the United Kingdom. In particular textiles and food, drink and tobacco play a far larger part than they do in the United Kingdom. Indeed these two industry groups account for 47 per cent of total output and with the addition of the engineering group the figure rises to 81 per cent. Clothing and footwear are likewise heavily represented; metal manufacturing and engineering as a whole are rather under-represented, so also is chemicals.

But although these figures show the composition of Scottish output to be much closer to the United Kingdom than either Wales or Northern Ireland, the alleged structural disadvantage of Scotland cannot be dismissed so lightly. In the first place, although the difference may not be as apparent as is commonly assumed, there is a heavy weighting of shipbuilding and textiles both of which tend to be slow growing industries both in Scotland and in the United Kingdom. There is a comparatively light representation of chemicals and vehicles, which are fast growing industries in the United Kingdom.[1]

In addition it must be remembered that the order groups of the Standard Industrial Classification contain a wide variety of trades. And there is evidence from the Toothill Committee's findings that Scotland's structural disadvantage becomes more apparent at the level of trades within orders.[2] Indeed, it seems to be one of the important features of the Scottish economy that the structural disadvantage is more apparent within orders than in comparisons

---

[1] These figures do not include the recent development of the motor vehicle industry in Scotland which took place after 1960.

[2] *Committee of Inquiry into the Scottish Economy*, op. cit., Appendix II.

THE OUTPUT OF MANUFACTURING INDUSTRY

between order groups. In this it differs from the other regions of the United Kingdom where the structural differences are more easily seen. Thus in Scotland vehicles until recently contained no motor car manufacture, and comprised mainly commercial vehicles with a heavy weighting of locomotive shops. Food, drink and tobacco in Scotland includes whisky manufacture; and textiles are primarily woollen and jute textiles. These are perhaps some of the more obvious differences, but they can arise in some degree or other in virtually any industrial order group.

THE GROWTH OF OUTPUT

The rates of growth are given in Table III. Since these can readily be obtained from published sources only selected years have been given. But it must be remembered in making the comparisons that the particular selection of years is of great importance. Different years which happened to be more favourable to any industry or any region would give rather different results.[1]

It will be seen that Scottish growth rates exceeded the United Kingdom between 1954 and 1960 only in engineering and electrical goods, textiles and clothing. Between 1954 and 1958 Scotland did better than the United Kingdom in chemicals, clothing, and bricks, pottery and glass. But in the earlier period, 1951 to 1954, Scottish rates of growth exceeded the United Kingdom in a considerable number of industries, and the rate of growth for manufacturing industry as a whole was the same for the two areas.

At first sight this appears to contradict the view that Scotland's poor rate of growth results from an insufficient share of the growing industries. Some of these industries, certainly are under-represented and this would contribute to a slow rate of growth. Moreover those industries in which Scotland had a large share, shipbuilding and textiles especially, tended to be either in decline or growing very slowly. But probably more important than this is the failure of those industrial orders which are growing fast in the United Kingdom to grow equally fast in Scotland. In the period 1954–1960 the fastest growing order groups in the United Kingdom were chemicals, vehicles, paper and printing, and other manufacturing industries. None of these grew at as fast a rate in Scotland as they did in the United Kingdom

[1] These comparisons are based on the Index of industrial production (*Digest of Scottish Statistics*, October 1963). The revised index gives a higher rate of growth to food, drink and tobacco, engineering and clothing; bricks, pottery and glass and timber and furniture have a lower rate (see note on the revised index, p. 136).

as a whole; and with the exception of chemicals their performance in Scotland was very poor. Some of this will undoubtedly be accounted for by Scotland's structural disadvantage within orders, already referred to. This is obviously true of vehicles. But it is remarkable that Scotland's performance is poorer than the United Kingdom's in so many order groups and it is hard to explain every order group in terms of a structural disadvantage.

At first sight this seems to imply that those sections of the growth industries which settled in Scotland were for some reason unable to keep up the growth rate achieved in the rest of the United Kingdom. It might be implied from this that there was something about the Scottish region which impeded growth.

However, growth comprises not only the expansion of existing firms but also the opening of new firms and the starting of branch factories and plant. Therefore, although Scotland's poor rate of growth could be explained by the failure of existing firms to do as well as in the rest of the United Kingdom, it could equally well be caused by an inadequate share of new firms starting up and of new branches and plant of existing British firms. This latter is the more conventional explanation and seems more likely to be the correct one.

OUTPUT PER PERSON EMPLOYED

Figures presented in Chapter 2 (Table V) showed that Scottish output per head in manufacturing was about 97 per cent of the United Kingdom level at the time of the 1958 Census of Production. The difference between Scotland and the United Kingdom is therefore small as regards productivity per head. On the other hand Wales had a higher output per head than the United Kingdom, being about 18 per cent above the latter; and the figure for Northern Ireland was much lower at only 68 per cent of the United Kingdom level.

In part this serves to illustrate in another way that Scotland's industrial structure bears more similarity to the United Kingdom's than does that of either Wales or Northern Ireland. Output per person employed varies greatly from one industry to another as the figures in Table IV show. For example the United Kingdom figures vary from an output per head of £1,656 in chemicals to £583 in clothing. Generally speaking, food, drink and tobacco, chemicals, metal manufacture, engineering, vehicles, and paper are the industries where output per head is highest and textiles, leather and clothing those where it is lowest.

To a considerable extent this explains the position of Wales and

Northern Ireland. With its heavy emphasis on metal manufacture, an industry with high output per person employed, Wales naturally tends to have above average output per person employed in manufacturing as a whole. Northern Ireland output is heavily weighted by textiles, and it is therefore not surprising that output per head for manufacturing as a whole is below the United Kingdom level.

This, however, is not the whole explanation. The figures in Table IV also show that output per person employed varies considerably between regions even industry by industry. Textiles provide the most striking example: here the output per person employed in Northern Ireland is only £491 compared with £1,519 in Wales. The reason for this is that Welsh textiles are primarily man-made fibres, while in Northern Ireland traditional textiles predominate.

Disparities also occur in the other industry groups though none are quite so large. The feature of the comparison which stands out most is that output per person employed in Northern Ireland is lower than in the United Kingdom for every order group with the one exception of 'other manufacturing'. In many cases the difference is substantial. It may be that this reflects the high level of unemployment in Northern Ireland, a tendency for earnings to be lower and for less emphasis to be placed on labour saving techniques than in the United Kingdom.

Wales on the other hand has a higher output per head than the United Kingdom in metal manufacture, engineering and electrical, textiles, leather and other manufacturing. Apart from the figure for textiles already referred to the high output in metal manufacture at £1,555 is of especial interest. This is £300 above the United Kingdom level. Presumably the difference results from the particular characteristics of the Welsh metal industry and the large part played by steel.

The Scottish figures are also above the United Kingdom level in a number of industries. These are food, drink, and tobacco, where whisky is probably responsible, chemicals, engineering, metal goods, leather, and bricks, pottery and glass. But in many of these the difference is small. On the other hand those industries which have output per head below the United Kingdom level are in most cases well above the Northern Ireland level.

It is noteworthy that in three of the industries which are more heavily represented in Scotland than in the United Kingdom, metal manufacture, shipbuilding and textiles, the Scottish output per head is below the United Kingdom level. No doubt this is responsible to a considerable extent for Scotland's slightly lower figure in manufacturing as a whole.

WAGES AND SALARIES IN MANUFACTURING INDUSTRY

In the previous chapter it was shown that profits, including income from self-employment, tend to form a higher proportion of Scottish gross product in some industries than they do in the United Kingdom as a whole. This tendency was less apparent in manufacturing than in a number of other industries, but it seemed to apply here also in 1958 though not in 1954. It was suggested that there might be a greater proportion of smaller firms with partners or working proprietors in Scotland and in consequence a smaller proportion of salaried staff. The separation of employment income into wages and salaries is not possible for all industries and services individually, but figures are available for manufacturing industry in 1951 and 1954 and for those other industries covered by the Censuses of Production. Figures for 1958 were unfortunately not published for Scotland in the 1958 Census. It will be seen from Table V that salaries do form a smaller proportion of Scottish employment income than they do in the United Kingdom as a whole. However, the difference is fairly small and not nearly so marked as it is for Northern Ireland or Wales.

THE OUTPUT OF MANUFACTURING INDUSTRY

TABLE I
SCOTLAND
Manufacturing Industry Net Output 1951–60*
£ million

1958 Standard Industrial Classification	1951	1952	1953	1954	1955	1956	1957	1958	1959	1960
Non-Metalliferous Mining Products, etc.	13·9	16·5	16·9	16·8	17·9	19·1	20·1	19·8	21·2	24·6
Chemicals & Allied	24·7	35·5	36·9	37·7	41·3	41·9	47·0	49·5	50·8	51·5
Metal Manufacture	56·6	50·8	50·5	48·0	54·9	60·2	61·8	63·6	62·1	77·3
Engineering, Shipbuilding & Electrical	119·5	127·6	133·5	152·7	165·9	171·8	188·4	206·6†	206·2†	214·5†
Vehicles	31·9	41·8	45·9	49·0	52·5	58·4	62·2	66·5	64·6	69·3
Metal Goods (N.E.S.)	17·3	18·9	16·8	18·6	23·4	25·0	27·1	24·5	26·3	28·6
Precision Instruments	4·0	4·3	5·0	6·4	6·9	6·4	6·8	—	—	—
Textiles	59·4	47·0	61·6	64·7	67·3	69·7	69·4	64·4	65·9	73·8
Leather & Leather Goods, etc.	2·3	2·4	2·8	3·1	3·1	3·0	3·1	2·9	3·1	2·7
Clothing	11·6	12·7	12·9	13·8	14·2	15·0	15·3	17·7	18·5	20·2
Food, Drink & Tobacco	73·8	76·7	81·1	88·5	96·3	102·4	107·7	126·0	131·0	138·6
Manufacture of Wood & Cork	14·5	14·9	15·9	16·4	14·8	15·7	16·3	15·4	15·1	15·5
Paper & Printing	39·5	29·1	33·4	41·9	44·9	45·1	46·0	49·3	49·8	54·3
Other Manfg.	11·7	8·9	12·2	13·5	13·6	13·3	14·3	13·6	14·6	16·0
Total Net Output	480·7	487·1	525·4	571·1	617·0	647·0	685·5	719·8	729·2	786·9
Contribution to Gross Domestic Product	437	439	472	510	560	585	628	639	656	708

* Adjusted to definitions used for 1954 Census of Production and to include repair trades.
† Including Order IX (Precision Instruments, etc.).

Note: The Methods used to construct this table are explained in detail in the Appendix, 'Sources and Methods', pp. 143–156.

TABLE II
Manufacturing Industry
Percentage Distribution of Net Output
1958*

	SCOTLAND	WALES	NORTHERN IRELAND	UNITED KINGDOM
Food, Drink & Tobacco	16·8	5·5	24·2	11·7
Chemicals & Allied	7·7	11·7	†	9·4
Metal Manufacture	10·0	39·5		8·8
Engineering & Electrical	21·4	11·3		22·2
Shipbuilding & Marine Engrg.	8·0	5·3‡	34·3	2·9
Vehicles	5·0			10·4
Metal Goods	3·5	5·9		5·6
Textiles	9·9	7·7	22·8	7·8
Leather	0·4	0·5	†	0·6
Clothing & Footwear	2·2	1·9	8·4	3·9
Bricks, Pottery & Glass	3·0	3·4	2·6	3·8
Timber & Furniture	2·4	1·4	1·8	2·7
Paper, Printing & Publishing	7·7	2·6	3·3	7·4
Other Manfg.	2·1	3·3	2·6†	2·9

* Using 1958 Standard Industrial Classification. Based on the net output figures of the 1958 Census of Production. Repair trades are not included and the percentages therefore do not correspond to the figures given for 1958 in Table I.

† Chemicals and Leather included in other manufacturing industry.

‡ Non-disclosed trades, percentage figure obtained by subtraction from total.

THE OUTPUT OF MANUFACTURING INDUSTRY

TABLE III
Growth of Manufacturing Output 1951–60
1954=100

	SCOTLAND			NORTHERN IRELAND			UNITED KINGDOM		
	1951	1958	1960	1951	1958	1960	1951	1958	1960
Food, Drink and Tobacco	89	108	116	94	141	169	93	109	117
Chemicals and Allied	92	122	135	*			84	115	141
Metal Manufacturing	100	90	107				93	101	123
Engineering and Electrical	94	110	118				91	112	115
Shipbuilding		100	83	79	98	114	96	109	92
Vehicles	73	90	92				80	118	139
Metal Goods	98	104	116				101	106	119
Textiles	93	91	102	104	92	109	100	87	96
Leather and Leather Goods, etc.	89	87	87	*			107	88	89
Clothing	103	105	126	93	107	130	96	102	121
Bricks, Pottery and Glass	80	101	114	90	129	192	94	98	114
Timber and Furniture	90	88	87	108	113	123	91	94	107
Paper, Printing & Publishing	97	101	112	90	126	163	91	111	133
Other Manufac. Industry	106	96	109	95	119	127	92	113	135
	92	102	109	92	108	118	92	107	123

* Included in Other Manfacturing Industry.
Sources: *Digest of Scottish Statistics.*
  Annual Abstract of Statistics.
  Reports on the Census of Production of Northern Ireland.

Note: See p. 136 for the implications of the revised index of industrial production.

TABLE IV
Output per Person Employed by Industries 1958
£ per head

	SCOTLAND	WALES	N. IRELAND	UNITED KINGDOM
Food, Drink & Tobacco	1,316	1,036	1,113	1,263
Chemicals & Allied	1,535	1,426	—	1,656
Metal Manufacturing	1,127	1,555		1,213
Engineering & Electrical	1,039	1,012		1,006
Shipbuilding, etc.	779	—	751	825
Vehicles	909	—		1,047
Metal Goods	954	889		931
Textiles	685	1,519	491	723
Leather & Leather Goods	806	875	—	796
Clothing	511	513	420	583
Bricks, Pottery & Glass	980	972	868	975
Timber & Furniture	741	632	758	835
Paper, Printing & Publishing	943	1,000	802	1,065
Other Manfg. Industry	858	944	944*	918
Total	974	1,194	684	1,009

* Including Chemicals and Leather.

Note: These figures are taken direct from the 1958 Census of Production and without any of the adjustments required to make them comparable with earlier years which were necessary for Table I (see Appendix).

TABLE V
Salaries as a Percentage of Employment Income*

	1951	1958
Scotland	21·8	23·1
Wales	19·6	21·1
N. Ireland	16·7	17·4
United Kingdom	24·2	24·8

Source: Census of Production for 1954 and *Censuses of Production for Northern Ireland.*

Note: * Excluding small establishments not covered by Census. Employment income comprises wages and salaries as shown by the Census.

CHAPTER 5

THE PRICES OF MANUFACTURING OUTPUT

OWING to the absence of official statistics very little is known about regional variations in prices within the United Kingdom. There are many important aspects of this subject, but such discussion as takes place usually centres round differences in the cost of living. Less attention has been paid to the prices of output.

It is with such prices that this chapter is concerned, but the subject is tackled from a rather limited angle. No attempt was made to assess regional variations in the prices of similar products to see whether there were any important regional differences. The basic information for this is not available, and results could therefore only be obtained after conducting a massive survey. Instead, this chapter attempts to compare the rate of price increase for the output of manufacturing industry in Scotland, Northern Ireland and the United Kingdom to see whether there are any significant regional differences.

The method adopted relies heavily on the index of industrial production to estimate output at constant prices. The results this produces are in some cases rather surprising and it is difficult to accept all the conclusions which emerge without question. This can only reflect on the accuracy of the index of industrial production; and if all the results of the chapter cannot be accepted as firm estimates of differing price trends, then they do provide the subsidiary function of testing the index of industrial production.[1]

Significant differences in the rate of price change of manufacturing output may be expected to result from the particular industrial structure of the regions. If there is inflation, the products of some industries rise more rapidly in price than those of others; and even if there is no *general* inflation the process of economic development is inevitably accompanied by changes in the price of some products relative to others. This arises partly because higher costs can be more effectively matched by higher productivity in some industries than in

[1] This study was based on the index before it was revised in October 1964. The implications of the new figures are discussed on p. 136.

others, and partly because higher living standards alter the pattern of demand. Therefore, depending on the location of industries which are inflation prone, the manufacturing output of some regions is likely to rise more rapidly in price than that of others.

RATES OF PRICE INCREASE FOR MANUFACTURING OUTPUT AS A WHOLE

In the absence of published figures on prices it is possible to make some estimate of relative price changes from a comparison of figures of output at current and at constant prices. The net output of manufacturing industry at current prices is taken from the reports of the Census of Production. Output at constant 1954 prices is constructed by multiplying the 1954 Census figure of net output in value terms by the index of industrial production for manufacturing industry based on 1954.[1] Since this is a volume index it should not be affected by price changes; and its application in this way to the census figure for 1954 should give figures for the other years at 1954 prices. From these two sets of figures price indices can readily be derived by dividing the figures for output at current prices by those for output at constant prices. To avoid all possible inaccuracy the calculations have only been made for years in which there was a full census of production. The last year covered is therefore 1958, but to give a longer period for comparison figures for 1948 were also included. The results are given in Table I. It would be interesting to apply this exercise to all the standard regions of the United Kingdom; but unfortunately indices of industrial production are available only for the United Kingdom, Scotland and Northern Ireland.

The calculations show that Scottish prices rose at much the same rate as United Kingdom prices from 1948 to 1954; but since 1954 have risen much more rapidly. Northern Ireland's prices on the other hand rose more rapidly than those of the United Kingdom from 1949 to 1951, but since then have risen more slowly. Between 1954 and 1958, for example, Scottish prices of manufacturing output rose 23 per cent compared with 18 per cent for the United Kingdom and 11 per cent for Northern Ireland. It is odd that there should be this sudden divergence between Scottish prices and United Kingdom prices after 1954, and equally surprising that in the earlier period, in sharp contrast to 1951–1958, Irish prices rose more quickly than

[1] *Reports on the Census of Production*, Summary volumes, 1954 and 1958, Board of Trade, H.M.S.O., London. *Report on the Census of Production of Northern Ireland, 1958*, Ministry of Commerce, H.M.S.O., Belfast. *Annual Abstract of Statistics*, H.M.S.O., London; *Digest of Scottish Statistics*, H.M.S.O., Edinburgh; *Digest of Statistics No. 19*, H.M.S.O., Belfast.

THE PRICES OF MANUFACTURING OUTPUT

TABLE I
Prices of Net Output of Manufacturing Industry
1954=100

	UNITED KINGDOM	SCOTLAND	NORTHERN IRELAND
1948	81	82	(1949) 79
1951	90	90	93
1954	100	100	100
1958	118	123	111

Sources: *Census of Production for 1954 and 1958* (United Kingdom) Summary Tables.
Census of Production for Northern Ireland, 1958.
Annual Abstract of Statistics 1958 and 1960; *Digest of Scottish Statistics*, 1960 and 1963.

Note: Census of Production Reports vary considerably in scope and coverage and considerable adjustment is necessary in making comparisons. In 1948 and 1951 Scottish figures cover larger establishments only and the U.K. figures are therefore taken on the same basis.

those of Scotland and the United Kingdom. If the rate of increase is related to the particular products produced, one would not expect the pattern to change except over a very long period.

There are a number of possible explanations for this. Controls were still widely used in this early post-war period; and it may be that they distorted the pattern of price increases. For example, it is conceivable that the particular industries sited in Scotland happened to be more subject to control than those sited in Northern Ireland. If this was so, the prices of Irish output might be expected to rise more rapidly.

In addition the particular selection of years in the comparison undoubtedly has the effect of magnifying the difference. Figures for Northern Ireland in 1948 are not available, while for Scotland and the United Kingdom a detailed Census of Production was taken in 1948 but not 1949. The United Kingdom figures suggest, however, that prices were slightly lower in 1949 than they were in 1948; this might account for a part, but by no means all, of the apparent difference in rates of increase during the earlier period.

Another point to emerge is that the price index for the United Kingdom calculated here rose 18 per cent between 1954 and 1958, whereas the official price index based on *sales* of output of manufacturing industry rose only 11 per cent over the same period.[1] This

[1] *Annual Abstract of Statistics*, 1960.

difference presumably arises because the official figures refer to sales of gross output including raw materials, fuel, etc. whereas the figures calculated here refer to net output only. For example, if the prices of raw materials were falling during the period (as they were in some cases), this would automatically give rise to a discrepancy between a price index based on gross output and one based on net output.

THE EFFECT OF INDUSTRIAL STRUCTURE ON RATES OF PRICE INCREASE

It would be interesting to discover the extent to which these differing rates of price increase can be associated with the industrial structure of the region. Variation in structure would seem to offer the most likely explanation of the differing behaviour of prices, since it would be surprising if the prices of *similar* products could move in such a

TABLE II
Price Increases by Industries 1954–58† (1954=100)

	U.K.	SCOTLAND	N. IRELAND	U.K.	PERCENTAGE DISTRIBUTION OF NET OUTPUT SCOTLAND	N. IRELAND
Food, Drink & Tobacco	129·9	131·7	107·4	11·7	16·8	24·2
Chemicals & Allied	118·9	107·6	*	9·4	7·7	*
Metal Manufacturers	127·8	147·5		8·8	10·0	
Engrg. & Electrical	119·5	122·1		22·2	21·4	
Shipbuilding & Marine Engineering	111·8	121·1	123·3	2·9	8·0	34·3
Vehicles	108·6	149·3		10·4	5·0	
Metal Goods	115·5	126·5		5·6	3·5	
Textiles	110·4	109·4	100·3	7·8	9·9	22·0
Leather	107·5	107·4	*	0·6	0·4	*
Clothing & Footwear	108·8	122·4	112·6	3·9	2·2	8·4
Bricks, Pottery & Glass	120·2	117·8	102·9	3·8	3·0	2·6
Timber & Furniture	122·5	106·8	125·9	2·7	2·4	1·8
Paper, Printing & Publ'ng	116·3	116·7	104·0	7·4	7·7	3·3
Other Manufacturing	109·7	114·8	99·3*	2·9	2·1	2·6
Total	117·8	123·1	110·8			
Total by applying U.K. rate of price increase to Scottish and Irish composition of output by orders	—	118·9	117·3			

Note: * Chemicals and leather are included with 'other manufacturing' industry for Northern Ireland.

† This table should be compared with the figures based on the revised index which gives very different results (see p. 136).

way as to cause substantial differences between regions of the same economy. One would therefore expect that those regions with a more rapid rate of price increase than the others could be shown to have a proportionately larger share of those order groups or trades which are subject to rapid price increases. Thus if the products of industry X rise more rapidly than the products of other industries, any region in which industry X plays a large part would tend to show a more rapid rate of price increase for manufacturing industry than the other regions.

Unfortunately it is impossible to carry out a thorough investigation of the structural factors: such a study would have to be conducted at the trade level of the Standard Industrial Classification, and at this level the information on prices is not available. In Table II, however, an analysis is made of the rate of price increase by industrial order groups. As the last chapter showed, the composition of the Scottish economy, as analysed by Orders, is actually not so very different from the United Kingdom as a whole. Shipbuilding, metal manufacture, food, drink and tobacco and textiles are admittedly more heavily weighted in Scotland than in the United Kingdom. But only two of these industries had a high rate of price increase in the United Kingdom. Chemicals and vehicles play a smaller part. But when analysed in this way the Scottish economy is certainly much closer to the United Kingdom than either Northern Ireland or Wales.

Indeed the main conclusion from Table II is that differences in structure *by industrial order groups* do not offer a satisfactory explanation of the differing rates of price increase for total manufacturing output either for Scotland or Northern Ireland. Applying United Kingdom rates of price increase by order groups to the actual weighting of Scottish output by order groups gives Scotland a hypothetical rate of price increase for total manufacturing output of 19 per cent between 1954 and 1958. This compares with the United Kingdom rate of 18 per cent and the actual Scottish rate of 23 per cent.

If the explanation still rests on structure, the important structural differences must therefore be at the level of trades within orders. At the level of industries as classified by orders the structural differences do not offer an adequate explanation. This is perhaps not surprising, since the order groups are so broad that one group may contain what are in effect widely differing industries. Thus the Scottish vehicle industry contained no motor car manufacture during the period in question, and the composition of such groups as textile and food, drink and tobacco varies tremendously from one region to another. As was noted in the last chapter, the evidence suggests that many of the most important structural differences between the United Kingdom and Scottish economies appear within rather than between the main order groups.[1] Unfortunately it is impossible to test the significance of this for price changes.

Nevertheless the comparison of rates of price increase by order in Table II yields some interesting results. The Scottish price rise is smaller than the United Kingdom's in chemicals, textiles, bricks, pottery, glass and timber and furniture. The differences are large for chemicals and timber and furniture. Leather is the only order group where the rates of price rise are approximately the same. For the remaining groups the Scottish rate is above the United Kingdom rate. Most remarkable are metal manufacture and vehicles: the estimated price increase in these industries was close to 50 per cent in Scotland between 1954 and 1958; while in the United Kingdom it was only 28 per cent for metal manufacture and 9 per cent for vehicles. It is clear that metal manufacture in Scotland differs considerably in character from the United Kingdom industry, as does the Scottish vehicle industry. But the figures do seem rather surprising. These two industries account for a substantial part of the disparity in the rates of price increase between Scotland and the United Kingdom. Indeed had they experienced price increases at the United Kingdom rate, Scotland's overall rate of price increase would have been 20 per cent, only 2 per cent above the United Kingdom rate compared with an actual 5 per cent.

The results for Northern Ireland are similar in so far as the rate of price increase for manufacturing output as a whole cannot be accounted for by the order group composition of the Irish economy. The economy of Northern Ireland differs considerably from both the United Kingdom and Scotland; and some industrial orders which play an important part in the two latter cases are absent from Northern Ireland completely. Even so if the Northern Ireland weighting by orders is applied to the United Kingdom rates of price increase, the total price rise for manufacturing industry would come to 17·3 per cent between 1954 and 1958. This compares with 17·8 per cent for the United Kingdom and Northern Ireland's actual rate of 10·8. The composition of output by orders therefore accounts for an even smaller part of the difference in the rates than it did for Scotland.

Comparing the Northern Ireland rates of price increase with those for the United Kingdom by industry, it will be seen that only for the

[1] *Report of the Committee of Inquiry into the Scottish Economy* (Toothill Report), Scottish Council (Development and Industry), 1961. Appendix 2.

group of engineering industries and timber and furniture is the Northern Ireland rate above that of the United Kingdom. The three engineering industries are taken together and the combined price increase is 23·3 per cent; the equivalent combined rate for the United Kingdom would be 15·5 per cent.[1] Apart from engineering the other two industry groups which play an important part in the Northern Ireland economy are textiles and food, drink and tobacco. For both of these the Northern Ireland rate of price increase is substantially below the United Kingdom rate. No doubt this may be partly accounted for by structure within these industry groupings. The textile group covers a wide range of industries and it happens that linen and cotton plays a large part in Northern Ireland just as woollen textiles account for a large part of the Scottish output and man-made fibres for the Welsh. Food, drink and tobacco is likewise a diverse group and the particular composition of Northern Ireland output may account for the slower rate of price increase.

CONCLUSION

According to the calculations in this chapter the prices of manufacturing output in Scotland rose more rapidly than in the United Kingdom between 1954 and 1958 although they had kept pretty closely in step from 1948 to 1954. Northern Irish prices on the other hand rose more slowly except in the immediate post-war years prior to 1951 when they seem to have risen more rapidly than in the United Kingdom.

Despite the peculiarity of some of the calculations, there is no reason to suppose that the general nature of these conclusions is anything but valid. This could well result from differences in economic structure within the main order groups which it was impossible to analyse. It is clear too that the rate of growth of the Scottish economy, even if measured by output at current prices, was below that of the United Kingdom after 1954. Wage rates on the other hand tended to keep more closely in step with the rest of the United Kingdom. Such a situation is bound to be inflationary; and one would expect that prices would rise more rapidly in Scotland.

It is certainly surprising that this tendency only became apparent after 1954. Since it most probably resulted from the basic character-

[1] This leaves out metal manufacture which is officially included with engineering in the Northern Ireland census but is assumed not to be of much importance. If it was included the combined rate of price increase for the United Kingdom would be 17·5 per cent.

istics of Scotland's economic structure, one would expect it to show itself also in the earlier period. It is just possible, however, that some change in economic conditions after 1954 took place which altered the pattern of inflation as between industries making some, which also happened to be heavily represented in Scotland, much more inflation prone in relation to the others than they had previously been. It may be that this was the same change in economic conditions as caused Scottish economic growth to start flagging behind the United Kingdom rate.

But even if this can be accepted, some of the detailed Scottish figures for the period 1954 to 1958 still seem rather extraordinary. The price increase of nearly 50 per cent in vehicles and metal manufacture during these four years is very difficult to accept; and it is surprising that so many industrial orders achieve a higher rate of price increase than their counterparts in the United Kingdom as a whole. It seems more likely that the index of industrial production, on which these calculations were based, itself contains some discrepancies or that the use made of it here is in some way illegitimate.

The index of industrial production is, of course, intended to be used primarily as an indicator, and an attempt to derive precise estimates of economic growth may therefore be misleading. It is based to a great extent on gross output and may therefore lead to discrepancies in deriving estimates of the growth of net output if the relationship of net and gross output changes. In fact, net output formed a slightly smaller proportion of gross output in 1958 than in 1954 for all three areas. The effect of this would be to make growth rates appear higher if measured in terms of gross output than if based on net. For Scotland and the United Kingdom the extent of this difference is insignificant; but for Northern Ireland it may be more important, where net output accounted for 28·5 per cent of gross output in 1954 and 26·3 per cent in 1958.[1] If the index of industrial production were based mainly on gross output, it might tend to show a slightly higher rate of growth than that actually achieved by net output. This in turn would make the Irish calculations in this chapter show a slightly lower rate of price increase than was the case, and so account for some of the discrepancy.

What this amounts to is that the index is not really as accurate as one would like for the sort of exercise which is built on to it in this chapter. But it is an inescapable conclusion that if one cannot accept the rates of price increase as estimated, the indices of industrial pro-

[1] The equivalent figures for Scotland were 35·7 and 35·3 per cent, and for the United Kingdom 36·1 and 35·8 per cent (*Census of Production Reports 1958*).

duction must be misleading. There is no obvious reason for rejecting the United Kingdom and Northern Ireland estimates; but some of the rates of price increase estimated for Scotland definitely seemed too high. If this is so, the Scottish rate of growth must have been more rapid than was shown by the index. In particular it seems that the index may have underestimated the rates of growth in vehicle production and metal manufacture. In fact the index shows the output of both of these industries to have fallen 10 per cent between 1954 and 1958. Therefore if the estimated rate of price rise is unacceptable, output must have declined less than 10 per cent.

Taking Scottish manufacturing output as a whole, if prices had increased at the United Kingdom rate of 18 per cent between 1954 and 1958 instead of the estimated rate of 23 per cent, this could only be reconciled with the Census of Production figures for net output at current prices if the growth rate had been 6·4 per cent. Even a 20 per cent price increase would imply a growth rate of 4·6 per cent. But the growth rate as shown by the index was only 2 per cent.[1] It would seem that this would have to be stepped up to at least 4 per cent if more realistic results are to be obtained. Considering the importance attached to the rate of economic growth and the central part it plays in discussion of the Scottish economic problem, the significance of such a revision in the official index would be obvious. It is particularly unfortunate that all estimates of economic growth have had to rely solely on this index. The estimates in this book are no exception. No matter how good this index is, it is after all only an indicator for which a high degree of accuracy would not be claimed. The best solution to this problem would require the provision of better information on Scottish prices. If official price indices were published, this would provide a useful check for the index and enable the rate of growth to be calculated with much greater accuracy. It would also provide a great deal of useful information on the Scottish economy.

[1] *Digest of Scottish Statistics No. 21*, April 1963. Some earlier editions of the Digest gave a growth of only 1 per cent for the same period. But it should be noted that the recent revision of the index, which was published after the above was written, gives a growth of 6 per cent (see page 136).

CHAPTER 6

PERSONAL INCOME IN THE STANDARD REGIONS OF THE UNITED KINGDOM

IF the estimates of gross domestic product, income from employment, gross profits, etc. and the output of manufacturing industry could have been extended to cover all the standard regions of the United Kingdom some valuable comparisons might have been made. Serious economic analysis of many of these regions has seldom been attempted and much useful information might come from a better knowledge of their economic circumstances. This information would be of value not only to those concerned with the problems of the English regions. The regions which have been covered in this study are among what have come to be called the 'less prosperous regions'; and their economic condition would appear in better perspective if it could be compared in detail with the other regions of the United Kingdom.

Unfortunately it is impossible to present estimates for the English regions in anything like the detail that was given in the last three chapters for Scotland, Wales and Northern Ireland. The reason for this is the much poorer coverage of these regions in the official statistics. The basic data from published sources is not even sufficiently adequate to enable an estimate of gross domestic product to be made in years when there was a full Census of Production. Quite possibly much of the data exists in the files of government departments in unpublished form, but it would be difficult for a private research worker to obtain access to it and no such attempt was made for the present study.

However, it is possible to make a number of interesting comparisons between personal income in each of the standard regions. The Inland Revenue publish from time to time a survey of personal incomes; the latest of these gives a breakdown both by region and by counties, and it is primarily on it that the comparisons made in this chapter are based.[1]

[1] *105th Report of the Commissioners of Her Majesty's Inland Revenue, for the year ended March 30, 1962.* Cmnd. 1906, H.M.S.O., London.

It should be emphasized that these figures refer to income *accruing to persons resident in* the regions in contrast to gross domestic product which concerns all income *arising within* the region. Income accruing to persons living in a region may come partly from outside, notably from the ownership of property and shares, while, on the other hand, part of the income arising within a region may eventually accrue to people living outside. At the national level these flows may be quite small, since most people hold the bulk of their property and investments in their own country; but they may acquire much greater significance for a region, and there is no reason why the outflow of income arising within the region to persons outside should balance the inflow. It may well be, therefore, that the domestic income of a region, in the sense of personal income arising within the region differs considerably from the personal income accruing to inhabitants of the region, just as gross domestic product may differ for the same reason from gross national product.[1]

The figures given in the Inland Revenue survey do not quite correspond to personal income as defined in national accounting practice. They exclude income which did not come within the scope of the inland revenue; they also use somewhat narrower definitions which give smaller figures than those published in official national income estimates. For example, in 1959–60 total personal income net of deductions in the inland revenue survey came to £15·3 million in the United Kingdom compared with £19·6 million for 1959 in National Income and Expenditure.[2] Income from employment assessed under Schedule E came to £11·8 million compared with £12·6 million for wages and salaries; income from self-employment assessed under Schedule D came to £1·19 million compared with £1·91 million. Income from property, interest and dividends came to £1·40 million in the tax assessments compared with £2·07 million. Furthermore, the regional figures are even less complete, since they exclude civil servants, the armed forces and seamen, all of which were assessed centrally and are shown separately in the report.

It would no doubt be possible to adjust the Inland Revenue figures

[1] This point is well illustrated by Miss Deane's estimates of income for Northern Rhodesia where income accruing to residents was not much more than half the income actually arising within the country. (Phyllis Deane, 'Measuring National Income in Colonial Territories', *Studies in Income and Wealth, Vol. Eight*, National Bureau of Economic Research 1946, pp. 147–74.) This is of course an extreme case; no region of the United Kingdom is likely to have such a large disparity as this, but the difference between the two definitions of income may be nevertheless important.

[2] *National Income and Expenditure 1961*, H.M.S.O.

in a variety of ways to bring them closer to personal income as defined in national accounting usage. One could even calculate figures for national income (or net national product) by adding to personal income thus adjusted some estimates for the undistributed profits of companies and for government income of various types. Such estimates, however, could only be made in a rather rough and ready fashion for most regions; and the allocation of public authorities' income in particular would raise conceptual as well as practical difficulties. For example, it is far from clear how the income of airlines should be apportioned between the regions and for other nationalized undertakings such as the railways, the lack of suitable figures makes apportionment difficult.[1] Undistributed profits of companies could presumably be apportioned between the regions according to receipts of interest and dividends, but if the proportion of profits which was undistributed varied between regions, this procedure too could give rise to error.

It was felt that there was little advantage in making such adjustments. For the purpose of drawing comparisons, most of the interesting points emerge from the Inland Revenue figures. Moreover, these figures can be regarded as reliable, whereas their reliability might be more questionable after going through the various processes required to alter their definition.

THE COMPARISON OF PERSONAL INCOME

Personal income, as assessed by the Inland Revenue, is given by regions in Table I. As already stated, the figures exclude incomes for seamen, members of public departments, and the forces, all of which were assessed centrally and are shown at the foot of the table. The figures for total income show the remarkable extent to which the London and South-Eastern region exceeds the others in importance. It appears that 27 per cent of total United Kingdom personal income accrues to London and the South-East, even after excluding the Public Departments, the majority of which happen to be located in this region. The regions next in importance in terms of income are the North-West, which accounts for 12 per cent, the Midland region which contributes just under 10 per cent and Scotland less than 9 per cent. Northern Ireland has the smallest income, amounting to only 1·7 per cent of the United Kingdom total.

When these figures are expressed per head of the total population

[1] See Appendix where this problem is discussed in relation to Scottish Gross Domestic Product. (Appendix, pp. 160–2.)

in each region (Table II) it is possible to give an approximate idea of their relative living standards. It should be remembered, however, that prices are far from uniform, and a region with a high income per head may not be as much better off as it seems. Nor does it necessarily follow that in a region with high average income per head the majority of the population are better off than in other regions. The average may be influenced by a comparatively small group with exceptionally high incomes. The importance of this could be assessed by examining the distribution of income by regions. Suitable material is available for such a study in the inland revenue reports, but it was not attempted here.

The figures in Table II show that London and the South-East has easily the highest average income per head, exceeding the United Kingdom average by 27 per cent; but prices are also likely to be higher in this region. The actual figure must be used with some caution for this particular region; but even if it exaggerates the true position, it is clear that the income per head of this region is well above the others.[1] Only one other region, the Midland, exceeds the United Kingdom average. But the Southern, North Midland, North-West and East and West Ridings are extremely close to the average. Northern Ireland's income per head is by far the lowest at only 63·8 per cent of the United Kingdom figure. The Scottish figure is 87·3 per cent, which is better than four other regions: the South-West 80·3 per cent, Wales 83·6 per cent, the Northern 86·8 per cent and Northern Ireland. The Eastern region is very close to the Scottish with 87·3 per cent of the United Kingdom income per head.

The really exceptional regions are therefore London and the South-East and Northern Ireland. The Scottish figure is certainly one of the lower ones, but the difference between it and the majority of English regions is not great. Scotland is commonly made to appear rather badly off by comparison with England as a whole. But this is because the figures both for England and for the United Kingdom are so greatly affected by the inclusion of London and the South-East which is an exceptional region.

It will be noticed that Scottish personal income per head at 87·3 per cent of the United Kingdom level is very similar to Scottish gross

---

[1] This figure is obtained by dividing the assessed income of the region by the resident population. Income tends to be assessed according to place of work rather than residence, and owing to the importance of travel to work in London and the South-East a discrepancy may arise. It is possible, therefore, that this calculation gives rather too high a figure of income per head in this region and too low a figure for the Eastern and Southern regions.

domestic product per head as a percentage of the United Kingdom. In 1959 this was 87·8 per cent.[1] It is tempting to try to draw conclusions from this. It would obviously be useful to know whether the income accruing to Scottish residents from outside was greater or less than the part of the Scottish domestic product going to persons not resident in Scotland. This would establish whether Scotland had a positive or negative net income from other regions and abroad.

Such income accounts for the difference between gross domestic product and gross national product as normally defined. National product will exceed domestic product if there is an inflow of net income from abroad. A comparison between these two variables for Scotland is not possible since gross national product is not calculated. But, as a percentage of the United Kingdom total, the figures for personal income per head are likely to be fairly similar to national income (or net national product) per head, since the missing components required to convert personal income per head as a percentage of the United Kingdom to national income per head are unlikely to have much effect on the ratio. However, a comparison of the personal income ratio at 87·3 per cent and the domestic product ratio at 87·8 per cent cannot be made to give satisfactory results. The difference between the two figures is insignificant and net income from other regions and abroad could only be obtained as a residual. The figures from which the residual would be calculated are large and subject to considerable margins of error so that any estimate which might be made of net income from other regions or abroad would be quite meaningless.

All that can be concluded, is that there is no enormous flow of income into or out of Scotland such as one sometimes finds in an underdeveloped country when a very large proportion of the capital assets are in foreign ownership. A satisfactory estimate for Scotland will have to be made by direct measurement, not as a residual; but sufficient data for such a measurement is not available.

Were it possible to make such calculations for each of the United Kingdom regions the results might prove to be very interesting. One might expect that net income from other regions and abroad would play a much larger part in the economy of regions than it customarily does for nations. For example, it would be surprising if those Scots holding shares in public companies had the bulk of their capital invested in Scotland. Probably most of it is in British companies but only a comparatively small part in companies and branches of companies operating in Scotland. Likewise those public companies which

[1] Chapter 2, Table II.

operate in Scotland may find that a large proportion of their shareholders live in regions other than Scotland.[1] The connection between the shareholders in a region and the particular companies operating in the region is therefore likely to be much less close than between shareholders and companies taking the country as a whole. For this reason there may well be very big differences between interest and dividends received by shareholders in a region and the dividend payments made by companies operating in that region. Net income from other regions and abroad may therefore be a much more important item in the income of regions than it is for the nation as a whole.

THE COMPOSITION OF PERSONAL INCOME

If the main components of total income are expressed per head of population, it will be seen that the composition varies considerably between regions. Earned income per head and investment income per head are both lowest for Northern Ireland, and highest for London and the South-East. But the South-West region, which has one of the highest investment incomes per head has the lowest earned income per head after Northern Ireland; and the Midland region, which after London and South-East has the highest earned income per head, has an investment income per head which is only half that of the Southern region. Scotland's earned income per head is one of the lower ones, exceeding only Northern Ireland, the South-West and Wales, although it is very close to that of the Eastern and Northern regions. Scotland's investment income per head, on the other hand, is one of the higher ones, being exceeded only by London and the South-East, the Southern region and the South-West (Table II).

If the figures are further subdivided as shown in Table III, it is possible to compare the relative importance of salaries, wages, property, etc. Profits and professional earnings seem to vary least, the range being from £19·6 per head of total population in the North-West to £26·5 in the South-West. Scotland with £24·9 per head exceeds the United Kingdom average of £22·9. Salaries vary much more: the figure for London and the South-East (excluding public

[1] The importance of this can be more easily estimated for Northern Ireland. Here Cuthbert found that 30·7 per cent of the paid-up capital of all companies with headquarters in Northern Ireland was attributed to shareholders outside Northern Ireland. For public companies the figure was as high as 72 per cent. By contrast residents of Northern Ireland held about 1·06 per cent of the capital of companies in Great Britain. (K. S. Isles and N. Cuthbert, *An Economic Survey of Northern Ireland*, H.M.S.O., Belfast, 1957, pp. 444-46.)

departments) at £126·1 per head is almost double that of any other region. Wales has the lowest salary income per head at £44·8. The Scottish figure of £54·9 is substantially behind the United Kingdom average of £71·0, but is higher than the figure for Wales, the Northern region, Northern Ireland, the South-West or the Eastern region.

Wages per head of total population vary from the Midland region with £175·0, which is the highest, to Northern Ireland with £81·1, which is by far the lowest. The Scottish figure, £126·7, is low and exceeds only Northern Ireland and the South-Western region. Wales does somewhat better than Scotland, though not as well as most of the English regions.

From Scotland's point of view property and investment incomes are in some ways the most interesting. Scotland's property income per head at £1·7 is by far the lowest of all; for example it is less than half the Welsh figure and less than 30 per cent of the London and South-East figure. The figures, of course, refer to *personal* income from property and therefore exclude local authority housing. Scotland's position is presumably explained by the very low level of rents and the comparatively small part played by private housing to let. These features of the Scottish housing situation are well known; but the comparison with the rest of the United Kingdom appears very strongly in these figures.

In contrast to property, Scotland has an income from interest and dividends per head which exceeds that of most of the other regions. The highest is again London and the South-East with £34·7 per head, the Southern region has £31·5, the South-West £24·3; Scotland has £20·0. By contrast Wales has only £11·6 and Northern Ireland £11·4. The Scottish figure is at first sight rather surprising though it bears out the results given by Professor Campbell in his earlier study of Scottish National Income.[1] Regional disparities of this kind can result from a tendency for wealthy people to congregate in particular areas of the country. They could also result from a higher propensity to save in some regions of the country which, if sustained for a long period of time, would tend to produce a high investment income. Probably both of these factors play a part, but which is the more important in offering an explanation it is difficult to say with any claim to accuracy.

[1] A. D. Campbell, op. cit. Campbell, however, found income from property and investments to be above the U.K. average per head in Scotland. This was not the case in the present study (see Tables II and III) though investment income was a higher proportion of total income in Scotland than in the United Kingdom.

THE STANDARD REGIONS OF THE UNITED KINGDOM

It may be that the high figure for the Southern region results from a tendency for wealthy people working in London to live in or retire to the Southern region. The reason for the high figure for the South-West is less clear, but it must also be influenced by the attractiveness of this region as a place for wealthy people to retire to. Scotland is much harder to account for. People who have made their wealth elsewhere certainly do settle in some of the more fashionable landowning parts of Scotland; but it is perhaps possible that a high propensity to save within Scotland also plays an important part.[1] If this is so, it would confirm the popular view of Scottish thrift. But, as will be shown below, the high investment income comes from a high income per person rather than a higher proportion of the total population with investment income.

Table IV presents in alternative form some of the more interesting features which emerged from Table III. Salaries as a percentage of net earned income vary from 39·6 per cent in London and the South-East to 20·4 per cent for the Northern region. Property income as a percentage of total net investment income varies from 27·3 per cent in Wales to 8·9 per cent in Scotland. A high ratio of course does not mean that property income is necessarily very high, but merely high in relation to other income from investment. The final column gives net investment income as a percentage of total income. The Southern region is highest with 11·8 per cent; the Northern region and Wales lowest with 5·3 and 5·4 per cent respectively. Scotland has 8·1 per cent which is higher than most English regions and higher than the United Kingdom average.

The figures so far presented have concerned either the absolute amount of income received in the regions or income per head of total population. As regards earned income, however, a low income per head of total population may result either from lower rates of payment per person in employment or from a lower proportion of the total population in employment. This latter factor is of considerable importance since the proportion of total population in employment varies considerably from region to region.

This is illustrated by the activity rates for the regions in 1959 given in Table V. It is unfortunately not possible to get figures for total manpower in employment including self-employed. The figures given therefore refer to total employees (including unemployed) as a percentage of total population. The unemployment percentages are also shown. The regions where the percentage of total male population in

[1] This is further discussed in Chapter 8 where expenditure and saving are analysed.

employment is lowest are Northern Ireland, the South-West, Wales, and Scotland. Scotland, however, is comparatively close to the United Kingdom level. For females, Wales has the lowest rate, followed by the South-West, the North and Northern Ireland.

It seems fairly clear, therefore, that the low earned income per head of total population in Northern Ireland, the South-West, Wales and the Northern region is at least to some extent a consequence of lower participation rates and is not entirely due to lower earnings per man employed.

These conclusions are confirmed by the figures in Table VI which show wages and salaries in the regions per insured employee. On this basis income in Northern Ireland is 83 per cent of the United Kingdom figure compared with 65 per cent (Table II) when measuring earned income per head of total population. The South-West is 87 per cent on this basis compared with 77 per cent, and Wales 102 per cent compared with 86 per cent. The Scottish figure is 90 per cent compared with 87 per cent. The difference between the figures in Scotland's case is much less marked because Scottish activity rates are not so far below the United Kingdom average.

The regions with the highest income per employee are London and the South-East with 110 per cent of the United Kingdom level, followed by the combined Southern and Eastern regions, the Midland region and Wales, all of which are above the United Kingdom average. Scotland, the South-West and Northern Ireland have the lowest earnings per employee. The case of Wales is interesting: though earned income per head of total population was rather low, income per employee is high, above the average for the United Kingdom. This was already noted in Chapter 3, and is mainly a consequence of Wales' industrial structure.[1] It may also be associated with the high ratio of male to female employment. Compared with Scotland it is interesting that Wales has a lower earned income per head of total population, but a substantially higher income per employee.

It was unfortunately impossible to relate profits and professional earnings to the occupied population or net earned income to total manpower including employees and self-employed. Figures for total manpower are published only for Scotland and Northern Ireland. As a rather inadequate substitute for this the figures were related to the number of cases assessed for tax. This is normally a lower figure than the occupied population owing to the practice of assessing husbands and wives together. If the difference between the number of

[1] Chapter 3, p. 39 and Table III.

cases assessed and the occupied population is similar for all regions, then this would furnish a guide to earned income per head of occupied population. But it is clear that substantial discrepancies could arise and the results must be interpreted with caution.

A surprising feature of the results is that Scotland has a very high income from profits and professional earnings per person assessed. Indeed the Scottish figure is second only to London and the South-East. Northern Ireland and Wales are by comparison very low. For earned income as a whole on the other hand Scotland is very low on the list, approximately equal to the South-West and exceeding only Northern Ireland.

In view of Scotland's very low property income in Table III property income per person assessed is not nearly as low as might be expected. This would appear to indicate that the predominant reason for the low property income is the absence of private houses to rent rather than a low income per unit of property.

Income from interest and dividends per person assessed is relatively high in Scotland, exceeding all regions except London and the South-East, the Southern and the South-West. Wales is the lowest. This would seem to imply that Scotland's high investment income is associated with a high income per person receiving it rather than a much higher proportion of people receiving investment income than in other regions. The same applies to the other regions with high investment income. In Scotland, for example, the number of cases assessed for inland revenue purposes under interest and dividends was below ten per cent of the United Kingdom total. Likewise the low investment income in Wales seems to be associated with a low income per person receiving it rather than a smaller proportion of the population having any investment income.

As a result of this high investment income, Scotland's total income per person assessed (including earned and investment income) is only slightly below Wales, but it is still the lowest income per person assessed after Northern Ireland.

CONCLUSION

The general picture which emerges from these calculations is that Scotland is one of the less well off regions in that total personal income per head of population is below average; but it is better than four other regions. In terms of earned income it does less well and earned income per employee is lowest after Northern Ireland and the South-West. Property income per head is the lowest of all; but investment income is comparatively high.

Of the other regions London and the South-East is better off than the others on almost every count and Northern Ireland worse off. The Midland region has a high earned income, but only a moderate investment income; the South-West has a high investment income but a low earned income. Wales has a high earned income per employee, but because of low activity rates, a low earned income per head of total population. The figures show that the characteristics of the regions differ considerably and sometimes surprisingly. It would be most interesting if at some future date each region's net income from other regions and abroad could be calculated to show the relative importance of interregional flows; it would be valuable too if the figures presented here could be compared with estimates of regional gross domestic product.

TABLE I
Personal Income by Regions 1959–60 £m.

	PROFITS AND PROF. E.	SALARIES	WAGES	PROPERTY	INTEREST & DIVIDENDS	NET EARNED INCOME	NET INVESTMENT INCOME	TOTAL	AS A % OF U.K.
London & S.-East	278	1,391	1,519	67	384	3,510	383	3,893	27·0
Eastern	86	196	462	15	61	805	64	869	6·0
Southern	67	178	360	15	87	663	89	752	5·2
South-West	89	176	337	16	81	661	84	745	5·2
Midland	93	313	812	17	74	1,327	75	1,402	9·7
North Midland	78	204	545	14	53	912	55	967	6·7
North-West	127	434	911	24	103	1,664	105	1,769	12·3
E. & W. Riding	82	248	638	14	66	1,070	67	1,137	7·9
Northern	65	150	472	10	39	735	41	776	5·4
England	966	3,288	6,053	191	947	11,347	963	12,310	85·3
Wales	63	118	355	9	30	576	33	609	4·2
Scotland	130	285	658	9	104	1,157	101	1,258	8·7
N. Ireland	32	68	114	4	16	233	17	249	1·7
United Kingdom	1,190	3,690	7,181	213	1,098	13,313	1,113	14,426	100
Seamen Public Dept. Forces	1·3	381	296	11	70	837	71	907	6·3

Note: Seamen, public departments and forces are excluded from the regional and national figures.

Source: 105th Report of the Commissioners of Her Majesty's Inland Revenue, Cmnd. 1906.

TABLE II
Income per Head of Total Population 1959–60

	NET EARNED INCOME £	INDEX	NET INVESTMENT INCOME £	INDEX	TOTAL £	INDEX
London & South-East	318·4	124·3	34·7	162·1	353·1	127·2
Eastern Region	224·9	87·8	17·7	82·7	242·7	87·5
Southern Region	242·0	94·5	32·4	151·4	274·5	98·9
South-West	197·8	77·2	25·1	117·3	222·9	80·3
Midland Region	285·9	111·6	16·2	75·7	302·2	108·9
North Midland Region	256·2	100·0	15·4	72·0	271·6	97·9
North-West	255·7	99·8	16·2	75·7	271·9	98·0
East & West Ridings	257·8	100·7	16·1	75·2	274·0	98·7
Northern Region	228·2	89·1	12·7	59·3	240·9	86·8
Wales	219·6	85·7	12·5	58·4	232·1	83·6
Scotland	222·8	87·0	19·5	91·1	242·2	87·3
Northern Ireland	165·3	64·5	11·9	55·6	177·1	63·8
England	265·3	103·6	22·5	105·1	287·9	103·7
United Kingdom	256·1	100·0	21·4	100·0	277·5	100·0

Notes: All income figures exclude income accruing to Civil Servants, Seamen or the Armed Forces. It was not possible to exclude these groups from the population figures.
Income is net of deductions as defined by the Inland Revenue.
Source: Cmnd. 1906 and *Annual Abstract of Statistics 1962.*

TABLE III
Types of Income per Head of Total Population 1959–60
£ per head

	PROFITS AND PROFESSIONAL EARNINGS	SALARIES	WAGES	PROPERTY INCOME	INTEREST AND DIVIDENDS
London & South-East	25·2	126·1	137·7	6·1	34·7
Eastern Region	23·9	54·7	128·9	4·1	19·0
Southern Region	24·3	64·8	131·2	5·5	31·5
South-West	26·5	52·5	100·7	4·6	24·3
Midland Region	20·1	67·5	175·0	3·6	16·0
North Midland Region	22·0	57·4	153·1	3·8	14·7
North-West	19·6	66·7	139·9	3·7	15·8
East & West Ridings	19·8	59·7	153·6	3·3	15·9
Northern Region	20·3	46·5	146·5	3·1	12·2
Wales	24·1	44·8	135·4	3·5	11·6
Scotland	24·9	54·9	126·7	1·7	20·0
Northern Ireland	22·6	48·3	81·1	2·7	11·4
England	22·6	76·9	141·6	4·5	22·1
United Kingdom	22·9	71·0	138·1	4·1	21·1

Note: Income above is not net of deductions as defined by Inland Revenue. The figures are therefore not exactly comparable with those in Table II. Income excludes all payments accruing to Civil Servants, Seamen and Armed Forces.
Source: Cmnd. 1906 and *Annual Abstract of Statistics 1962.*

TABLE IV
Relative Importance of Salaries, Property & Investment Income

	SALARIES AS % OF NET EARNED INCOME	PROPERTY AS % OF NET INVESTMENT	NET INVESTMENT INCOME AS % OF TOTAL
London & S.-East	39·6	17·5	9·8
Eastern	24·3	23·4	7·3
Southern	26·8	16·9	11·8
South-West	26·6	19·0	11·2
Midland	23·6	22·6	5·4
North Midland	22·4	23·4	5·7
North-West	26·1	22·9	6·0
East & West Ridings	23·2	20·9	5·9
Northern	20·4	24·4	5·3
Wales	20·5	27·3	5·4
Scotland	24·6	8·9	8·1
Northern Ireland	29·2	23·6	6·7
England	30·1	19·5	7·8
United Kingdom	27·7	19·1	7·7

TABLE V
Activity Rates and Unemployment by Regions (1959)

	LABOUR FORCE* MID 1959 '000s	ACTIVITY RATES PER CENT† MID 1959 MALES	ACTIVITY RATES PER CENT† MID 1959 FEMALES	UNEMPLOYMENT PER CENT DEC. 1959
London & S. Eastern / Eastern & Southern	7,806	78·4	39·6	1·2
Midland	2,145	82·1	40·7	1·0
E. & W. Ridings	1,847	80·2	37·8	1·5
North-West	2,961	79·8	41·3	2·2
Northern	1,298	77·0	31·1	3·3
North Midland	1,500	76·7	34·8	1·3
South-West	1,217	66·5	29·6	2·2
Scotland	2,145	76·5	36·6	4·3
Wales	951	69·4	26·2	3·3
Northern Ireland	476	63·0	33·3	7·1
United Kingdom	22·346	77·0	37·2	2·0

* Insured employees only, excluding self-employed and Armed Forces.
† Insured employees as percentage of total population over 15 years of age.
Sources: Ministry of Labour Gazette 1960.
Annual Reports of the Registrar-General.

TABLE VI
Income per Employee
Wages and Salaries

	£ PER INSURED EMPLOYEE	INDEX
London & S.-East	553·2	110·1
Eastern Region } Southern Region }	538·5	107·1
South-West	438·8	87·3
Midland Region	533·9	106·2
N. Midland Region	508·8	101·2
North-West	467·7	93·1
E. & W. Ridings	487·1	96·9
Northern Region	495·2	98·5
Wales	511·9	101·9
Scotland	451·2	89·8
N. Ireland	417·4	83·0
England	513·8	102·2
United Kingdom	502·6	100

Note: Neither Income nor employees from National Government Services and Sea Transport are included.

Source: Cmnd. 1906.
        Ministry of Labour Gazette.
        Digest of Scottish Statistics.
        Digest of Welsh Statistics.
        Digest of Statistics (Northern Ireland).

TABLE VII
Income per Person Assessed for Tax
£ per assessment

	PROFITS AND PROFESSIONAL EARNINGS	PROPERTY	INTEREST AND DIVIDENDS	NET EARNED INCOME	NET INVESTMENT INCOME	TOTAL NET INCOME
London & S.-East	850·7	44·0	407·2	745·3	417·0	811·8
Eastern Region	728·8	35·9	286·7	673·8	295·1	715·6
Southern Region	730·6	39·4	390·1	663·9	394·7	732·9
South-West	688·9	37·9	331·0	629·5	336·4	690·5
Midland Region	745·2	29·0	236·0	717·2	273·7	751·7
N. Midland Region	705·2	29·7	205·9	683·1	233·9	718·1
North-West	698·2	29·5	239·6	673·0	246·2	708·5
E. and W. Ridings	714·9	27·0	227·0	675·3	261·9	711·5
Northern Region	750·7	30·0	206·0	655·4	240·0	686·0
Wales	635·1	26·9	196·7	649·3	195·7	678·4
Scotland	840·9	27·3	303·1	628·7	368·8	674·6
N. Ireland	527·4	31·0	253·9	566·8	235·9	600·2
England	748·2	34·3	305·1	695·4	317·3	743·7
United Kingdom	742·1	33·2	295·8	684·2	308·1	731·7

Source: Cmnd. 1906.

CHAPTER 7

PERSONAL INCOME IN THE MAIN REGIONS AND COUNTIES OF SCOTLAND

PREVIOUS chapters have been concerned with income in Scotland as a whole; but the distribution of income within Scotland is also of considerable interest. The economic performance of different areas in Scotland tends, most commonly, to be thought of in terms of unemployment percentages, simply because these are the statistics most readily obtained. But figures for income by counties give a different and rather revealing picture of the pattern of prosperity.

The analysis of income within Scotland presented here is based on the income surveys of the Commissioners of Inland Revenue, as was the regional analysis in the last chapter.[1] Since 1950 these surveys have been made approximately every five years; but the most recent report contains more detailed information than its predecessors, and it is on it that the analysis of this chapter is based. The Inland Revenue report gives figures for Scotland both by regions and by counties. The regional analysis, which divides Scotland into the Clydeside conurbation, the North and South, gives rather more detailed information than the county analysis. Moreover, even the county analysis brackets a large number of the counties together, since the numbers involved are too small to make separate presentation possible.

INCOME BY REGION

The figures for the three main regions are presented in Table I. The Clydeside conurbation is as defined in the reports of the Registrar-General for Scotland; it includes Glasgow and parts of Lanarkshire, Renfrewshire and Dumbartonshire.[2] South Scotland comprises the remainder of the mainland counties south of Stirling including Edinburgh; and north Scotland includes all the remainder. The

[1] 105th Report, Cmnd. 1906, op. cit.
[2] Ibid., p. 36, and *Annual Report of the Registrar-General for Scotland 1959*, No. 105, p. 43.

assessments are made in relation to a person's place of work not his residence and the figures show all forms of personal income accruing to people in the regions defined in this way. As in the last chapter the figures refer to income received not income generated in the regions; this difference may be substantial especially for income from investments.

The figures for total personal income show that Clydeside has the largest income of the three regions. Investment income, however, is low and plays a proportionately smaller part in the total. Indeed, whereas investment income accounts for about 10 per cent of the total personal income in the South and 9 per cent in the North, in Cyldeside it accounts for less than 6 per cent. To some extent this is due to the low personal income from property in Clydeside which is less than half the figure for either of the other two regions; but the income from interest and dividends is also markedly lower. Property income no doubt reflects the high proportion of local authorities' housing and the low level of rents in Clydeside. In consequence of this, the percentage of privately owned housing is likely to be small and the personal income arising from it low.

Considering that Clydeside is predominantly an urban area while the other two are to a much greater extent rural, it may be thought that this difference in the role of property income is to be expected. But the comparisons made in the last chapter showed that some British regions which were predominantly urban had property incomes which formed a much larger proportion of total income than was the case for any of the Scottish regions. For example, in no English region, Wales or Northern Ireland did property income fall below 1 per cent of total personal income; in many regions it was nearer 2 per cent. Yet in Scotland only in the North does property income approximate to 1 per cent of the total.

The figures for earned income show a different pattern. Clydeside has by far the largest total of both wages and salaries. But in profits and professional earnings the North has the largest total and Clydeside the lowest. Salaries form the highest proportion of net earned income in Clydeside, 28 per cent, as against 25 per cent in the South and 20 per cent in the North. No doubt the high profits and professional earnings in the North reflect the large part played by agriculture, the tourist trade and fishing. In all of these industries income from self-employment which is assessed under profits and professional earnings, plays an important part.

The figures for income per head of total population show Clydeside to be better off than the other two regions. However, this result must be accepted with some caution, since the population figures are based on place of residence, while the income figures are assessed by place of work, as already stated. Consequently, if a large number of people travel into the Clydeside region to work, this could upset the reliability of the figures and cause Clydeside to have an apparently higher income per head than was justified. The Clydeside region is of course defined to include the bulk of the towns from which commuters regularly travel; but no doubt a certain amount of error is still bound to arise in this way.

As might be expected from the figures already outlined, investment income per head is much higher in both the North and the South than in Clydeside, while earned income per head is higher in Clydeside. Salaries and wages per head are again higher in Clydeside and profits and professional earnings are highest in the North. The difference between Clydeside and the North in both salaries and profits and professional earnings per head are very marked.

The last part of Table I gives income divided by the total number of cases assessed for tax. This is not subject to the difference of definition between residence and work which is involved when estimating income per head of total population. But the number of cases assessed for tax corresponds neither to the total population nor the working population, since husbands and wives are commonly assessed together. Broadly speaking the regional pattern is the same as for income per head of total population except that total income per person assessed is slightly higher for the South than for Clydeside, This contradicts the pattern found by taking income per head of total population. The reason for this is that the number of cases assessed form a higher proportion of total population in Clydeside than in the other two regions. Most probably this reflects a higher working population as a percentage of the total. This probably results from a more favourable age distribution of the population or a larger proportion of the women in employment. But if commuters from outside Clydeside formed an important element this could also explain the difference. Unfortunately it is quite impossible to assess the importance of this. It would be very much more satisfactory to be able to derive income per head of the working population and compare this with income per head of total population. But in the absence of figures for working population in 1959 this again is impossible.

The conclusions which emerge are therefore as follows: Clydeside has easily the highest income from employment, but income from investments including property is much lower than for either of the other two regions; income from self-employment, profits and professional earnings is highest in the North and lowest in Clydeside. The figures for total personal income per head show Clydeside 11 per cent above the Scottish average, the South 3 per cent below and the North 8 per cent below, but owing to definitional differences in population and income figures these results cannot be accepted with full confidence. Income per person assessed is slightly lower in Clydeside than in the South and lowest in the North. It seems likely that a higher proportion of the total population may be in employment in Clydeside than in either of the other regions. Therefore, although income per head of total population is highest in Clydeside, this may not reflect a higher income per head of working population, but rather a higher participation of total population in employment.

INCOME BY COUNTIES

The figures for income by counties in the Inland Revenue reports are rather less detailed than those for regions. Moreover, some of the counties were grouped together because the numbers involved were so small. As a result all of the northern counties including the northern islands have to be taken together. The same applies to a number of southern counties and certain others. In deriving figures for income per head of total population, the same problems of definition arise as occurred in the previous section. Income is assessed according to place of work while population is defined according to residence. If a large proportion of people lived in one county and worked in another, therefore, this could seriously undermine the reliability of the figures. It was thought that this problem was unlikely to assume serious proportions except in the case of Dumbarton, Renfrew and Lanark, which contain the Clydeside conurbation and are therefore shown combined as well as separately.

The figures for total income per head show a wide range from West Lothian which is the poorest to Renfrew which is the richest. If Renfrew is discounted as being part of the Clydeside conurbation, then Midlothian is the richest county. West Lothian does badly on all counts. It has a very low income from employment per head of total population, exceeding only the northern group and Argyll and Bute; it has the lowest profits and professional earnings and by far the lowest income from investment. Total income per head is only 65 per cent of the Scottish level. The northern group, which is the next poorest, have a high income from profits and professional earnings and a modest income from investment; total income is 75 per cent of the Scottish level. Argyll and Bute which like the northern group has an extremely low income from employment redeems this to some extent by having the second highest investment income per head and a high income from profits and professional earnings. Aberdeen, Banff, Moray and Nairn, which in terms of total income per head are not much better than Argyll and Bute, have a higher income from employment but a lower investment income.

The distribution between income from employment and profits and professional earnings naturally reflects the predominant occupations in each county. A low income from employment, therefore, does not necessarily point to a low income per employee; quite possibly it indicates a low proportion of employees and a high proportion of self-employed who are assessed under profits and professional earnings. Those counties where agriculture, the tourist trade and fishing play a large part fall into this category. It is therefore interesting to note that in almost all the counties where employment income is low, income from profits and professional earnings is high. The most important exception to this rule is West Lothian.

Approximately half of the counties or groups of counties have a total income per head which is between 90 and 100 per cent of the Scottish level. Once again they vary from Perth, the Berwick group and the Dumfries group, which have a fairly low income from employment but high income from investment and profits and professional earnings, to Stirling, Fife, Clackmannan and Kinross, and Ayr which have higher employment incomes but lower incomes from other sources.

The counties where total income per head exceeds the Scottish average are the Clydeside group, Angus and Kincardine, and Midlothian. The combined Clydeside counties with income per head 4 per cent above the Scottish average have a very high income from employment; but income from investment and profits and professional earnings are both substantially below the Scottish average. Angus and Kincardine, on the other hand, have a high income from investment and profits and professional earnings, though not as high as counties like Perth or Argyll and Bute; but income from employment is below the national average. Indeed the reason that Angus and Kincardine have a total income per head above the Scottish average is that they combine a moderate income from employment, similar to Ayr or Fife with a reasonably good income from investment and profits. Other counties may be as good or better under each category of income but do not have such a good all-round result.

Midlothian has an outstandingly high income from employment per head, one of the highest investment incomes and an income from profits and professional earnings which is not far from the average. The high total income per head is therefore the result of a good or outstanding income under each category just as West Lothian's low income went with a low income under all categories.

Another feature shown in Table II which is worthy of attention is the remarkably high proportion of Scottish total income which is accounted for by Clydeside. It will be seen that Lanarkshire accounts for 32 per cent of all Scottish personal income, while Lanark, Renfrew and Dumbarton combined, make up 43 per cent. This is a very high proportion of the total and it illustrates the remarkable extent to which Clydeside dominates the Scottish economy. Indeed Clydeside is of more importance to the Scottish economy than London and the South-East region, with 27 per cent of United Kingdom income, is to the country as a whole.

To many people some of the results of this survey may seem surprising. Probably most people if asked would assume that the Highland counties were the poorest in Scotland, and few would think of West Lothian. Possibly if the northern group could be split up one of them would turn out to have the lowest income. In some measure this may be the consequence of assessing personal income *accruing* to people in each county rather than income *arising* within each county. Admittedly West Lothian would probably have a low income on almost any basis. But the relatively good position of many other counties is the result of a high investment income. One may assume that much of this investment income is earned on assets held outside the county and that in many cases the income flowing into the county in this way exceeds the outflow to external owners of assets held within the county. One cannot be certain of this, since some of the Highland counties have a substantial income from distilling which flows to shareholders outside the county. But it is probable that an estimate of income arising within the county would show such counties as Perth, Argyll and Bute, the Berwick group and the Dumfries group in a less favourable light. Since there are no suitable statistics available, it is unfortunately impossible even to guess at the pattern which might emerge if income could be defined as domestic income; but it would make a most interesting comparison with the figures presented in this chapter. A recent study of Irish county income shows that personal income accruing to residents is in many cases much higher than income arising within the counties.[1] In some cases

---

[1] It is interesting to compare the county figures in this chapter with those for the Irish Republic (see E. A. Attwood and R. C. Geary, *Irish County Incomes in 1960*, Economic Research Institute, Dublin, paper No. 16). The Irish figures are

THE MAIN REGIONS AND COUNTIES OF SCOTLAND

personal income exceeded income arising by as much as 30 or 40 per cent. No doubt similar differences would be found to apply to the Scottish counties if the comparisons could be made.

---

not strictly comparable since personal income in this study includes income not covered by the British Inland Revenue, but it is noteworthy that total personal income per head ranges from £231 in County Dublin to £153 in Counties Mayo and Donegal.

TABLE I

Personal Income in the Main Regions of Scotland

	SALARIES	WAGES	PROFITS & PROFESSIONAL EARNINGS	PROPERTY	INTEREST AND DIVIDENDS	NET EARNED INCOME*	NET INVESTMENT INCOME*	TOTAL*
				£ million				
Scotland†	285·1	658·0	129·5	8·9	103·9	1,156·7	101·0	1,257·7
Clydeside	126·9	263·8	34·6	1·6	28·9	457·2	27·5	484·7
South	83·4	187·6	38·9	3·5	37·6	333·6	36·7	370·3
North	74·8	206·6	56·0	3·9	37·5	365·8	36·8	402·6
			£ per head of total population					
Scotland†	54·9	126·7	24·9	1·7	20·0	222·8	19·5	242·2
Clydeside	70·6	146·7	19·2	0·9	16·1	254·2	15·3	269·5
South	52·7	118·5	24·6	2·2	23·8	210·8	23·2	234·0
North	41·3	114·1	30·9	2·2	20·7	202·0	20·3	222·3
			£ per case of total tax assessments‡					
Scotland†	152·8	352·8	69·4	4·8	55·7	620·3	54·2	674·4
Clydeside	177·8	369·7	48·4	2·2	40·5	640·7	38·5	679·2
South	153·8	346·0	71·7	5·5	69·3	615·3	67·7	683·0
North	122·8	339·2	92·0	6·4	61·5	600·6	60·4	661·1

Note: * The last three columns are net of deductions as defined by the Inland Revenue.
† The Clydeside conurbation comprises parts of Lanarkshire, Dunbartonshire and Renfrewshire making an estimated population in 1959 of 1,798,464. South Scotland comprises the remainder of the mainland South of Stirlingshire including Edinburgh, with a total population of 1,582,525 in 1959. North Scotland includes all the remainder and had a total population of 1,810,671 in 1959.
‡ Total cases assessed for tax are those shown for net total personal income in the Inland Revenue Report.

Sources: 105th Report of the Commissioners of Her Majesty's Inland Revenue.
Annual Report of the Registrar-General for Scotland 1959. No. 105.

TABLE II
Personal Income per Head of Total Population by Counties

	INCOME FROM EMPLOYMENT	PROFITS & PROFESSIONAL EARNINGS	INCOME FROM INVESTMENT	TOTAL NET INCOME	INDEX	% OF TOTAL SCOTTISH INCOME
			£ per head			
Caithness, Inverness, Orkney, Ross & Cromarty, Sutherland & Zetland	116·9	39·7	15·5	180·8	74·7	3·1
Argyll & Bute	117·4	41·0	32·5	200·9	83·0	1·1
Aberdeen, Banff, Moray & Nairn	142·7	41·8	19·4	216·0	89·2	7·4
Angus & Kincardine	174·0	29·2	26·8	253·6	104·7	6·2
Perth	147·3	41·2	37·2	236·9	97·8	2·4
Stirling	193·7	18·0	13·4	238·0	98·3	3·7
Fife	176·9	19·7	14·8	219·4	90·6	5·7
Clackmannan & Kinross	188·3	18·6	14·4	240·0	99·1	0·9
Midlothian	220·3	23·5	31·1	289·7	119·6	13·3
West Lothian	133·0	11·7	4·3	157·5	65·0	1·2
Berwick, East Lothian, Peebles, Roxburgh & Selkirk	134·5	43·1	29·6	223·4	92·2	2·8
Dumfries, Kirkcudbright & Wigtown	140·3	44·6	29·3	226·8	93·6	2·7
Ayr	176·0	24·4	19·8	231·6	95·6	6·3
Dunbarton	181·8	12·7	16·1	223·5	92·3	3·2
Renfrew	240·1	20·2	20·0	296·1	122·2	7·9
Lanark	202·2	18·0	13·5	247·0	102·0	32·0
Dunbarton, Lanark, Renfrew Combined	206·5	17·9	14·7	252·7	104·3	43·2
Scotland	184·4	24·9	19·5	242·2	100	100

Sources: 105th Report of the Commissioners of Her Majesty's Inland Revenue.
Annual Report of the Registrar-General for Scotland 1959. No. 105.

CHAPTER 8

CONSUMERS' EXPENDITURE IN THE STANDARD REGIONS

INFORMATION on expenditure by regions during the period with which this book is concerned is far less adequate than one would wish. Ideally it should be possible to compile estimates of gross national product from the expenditure side to compare with those built up by the income and product methods. To prepare an integrated set of accounts such as this is, however, impossible with the data presently available. One therefore has to be content with a survey of consumers' expenditure.

Details of consumers' expenditure are available from the sample surveys of the Ministry of Labour.[1] It is on these reports that the present chapter is based; but the analysis has to be confined to 1953–54 and 1961–62, the only years for which regional figures were published.

Table I gives the results for 1953–54, expenditure per head being expressed as a percentage of the United Kingdom level. Perhaps the most important determinants of the pattern of expenditure are the level of income, the distribution of income and the size of household. In Northern Ireland's case, the high proportion of the population dependent on agriculture for a livelihood probably also has a considerable effect on the pattern of expenditure, especially as regards housing and food.

The pattern of expenditure differs considerably between regions, but in most cases it is difficult to attribute the differences to any one of the above factors. In particular it did not seem possible to distinguish any clearly defined pattern which applied to the low income regions as distinct from that which prevailed in the remainder.

The figures show that Scotland and Northern Ireland both have a low expenditure on housing, alcoholic drink and durable goods. Scotland has a high level of expenditure on tobacco, while Northern Ireland has high expenditure on fuel and light and clothing. Some of

[1] *Report of an Inquiry into Household Expenditure in 1953–54*, H.M.S.O., 1957. *Family Expenditure Survey: Report for 1962*. H.M.S.O., 1963.

these figures are clearly related to the size of households, which are above the national average in both regions, especially in Northern Ireland. For example, the high expenditure on clothing in Northern Ireland is probably associated with the high proportion of children. But even if expenditure is taken per household the outlay on housing and alcoholic drink still seems to be very low. On this basis Scottish expenditure on housing comes to 76·9 per cent of the United Kingdom level and Northern Irish to 73·2. For alcoholic drink the figures are 84·3 and 64·4 per cent respectively.

Other regions which were shown to have low incomes in Chapter 6 have very different expenditure patterns. The South-West has, like Scotland, a low expenditure on alcoholic drink and durable goods, but expenditure on housing is high. Wales has a remarkably high expenditure on durable goods which may perhaps coincide with some temporary situation such as the spread of television transmission at the time the survey was taken. Neither is any set pattern apparent for the regions with high income. London and the South-East has high expenditure on housing, on services and on transport. But the Midland and North Midland regions both show exceptionally high expenditure on alcoholic drink.

The income tax figures reveal wide differences between the regions. Contributions to income tax will depend partly on the level of income and partly on its distribution, the existence of a few supertax payers offsetting the low tax payments which would result from incomes which were below average in the rest of the region. The figures show that Northern Ireland and Scotland both have income tax burdens which are well below the national average. By comparison London and the South-East and the Midland region make large tax payments per head. Some of the other results are, however, quite unexpected. The highest tax burden of all is apparently in the South-Western region, which has a comparatively low income (see Chapter 6, Table II); and the Southern region which has a high income has a tax burden which is lower than Scotland. The South-West certainly has a high investment income and therefore presumably has a high proportion of super tax payments, but the same is true of the Southern region. One would clearly need to have much more information about this before being able to offer any explanation.

The figures for total expenditure show London and the South-East, the East and West Ridings, the North-West and Wales to have expenditure per head above the national average. The lowest levels of expenditure are those for Scotland, the Northern region and Northern Ireland. The regional pattern of expenditure may differ considerably from that of income owing to differences in the burden of taxation and in regional propensities to save. But even allowing for this the pattern of expenditure differs substantially from that shown by the personal income figures in Chapter 6. Since the income figures refer to 1959–60, one obviously cannot attach any significance to small differences in the proportions. But in Northern Ireland personal income was only 63·8 per cent of the United Kingdom figure; and outlay, including income tax and national insurance came to 85·1 per cent. In Wales income was 83·6 per cent and outlay is 100·5 per cent. The South-West and the Eastern regions likewise have outlays which as a proportion of the United Kingdom level greatly exceed the income proportion. The only regions where the income proportion exceeds the outlay proportion are London and the South-East, the Southern region and the Midland region. This result is perhaps not unexpected, since these were the three regions with the highest income per head according to the 1959–60 figures of the Inland Revenue Survey.

Various items of saving were included in the survey under 'other items recorded'; but the pattern is not consistent with what one would expect from examining income and expenditure. According to these figures such savings were above the national average in London and the South-East, the North-West and the South-West; Wales, Scotland and Northern Ireland had the lowest figures. It seems likely that these figures do not represent all savings and that they include the purchase of various types of investment which are made possible by the sale of other investments, as well as those which represent a net saving out of income. It would seem unwise therefore to accept these figures as illustrating differences in the propensity to save as between regions.

The expenditure figures for 1961–62 (see Tables II and III) are less satisfactory than those for 1953–54 in that the English regions are taken in groups and some of their more interesting characteristics are therefore concealed. Unfortunately no figures were published for Northern Ireland since the sample was too small to give meaningful results. On the other hand the survey did provide income figures which could be compared with those for expenditure.

As regards the pattern of expenditure, the figures show that in 1961–62 Scotland still had a low expenditure per head on housing, alcoholic drink and durable goods, but those figures are not so far below the national average as in 1953–54. On the other hand expenditure on transport, which was almost up to the national average in 1953–54, has fallen much further behind. Tobacco expenditure is still the highest of any region.

CONSUMERS' EXPENDITURE IN THE STANDARD REGIONS

The Welsh figures show a remarkable change from 1953–54. In particular the very high expenditure per head on durable goods in the earlier year has now fallen to a level which is only 84 per cent of the figure for Great Britain. Total expenditure is now more in line with the income level and it seems likely, therefore, that the 1953–54 figures were exceptional.

The main purpose of comparing the expenditure figures with those for income is to try to get some indication of savings in the regions. Income as defined in the survey includes state benefits and allowances; it is therefore not directly comparable with personal income as defined by the Inland Revenue and analysed in Chapter 6. Disposable income can be obtained by subtracting payments made to income tax and national insurance contributions from the income figures in the survey. It should then be possible to estimate savings by subtracting total expenditure from disposable income. Unfortunately it was impossible to have very much faith in this procedure since both the income and expenditure figures may be subject to a margin of error which would make the estimation of savings as a residual highly inaccurate. Moreover, it appeared that for every region total expenditure plus 'other recorded items' exceeded the figure for disposable income.[1] The difference ranged from as much as 40/- a week in London and the South-East to 16/- for Scotland and 12/- in the North Midland, Midland and Eastern group. If 'other recorded items' are excluded, disposable income is still short of total expenditure in London and the South-East.

This is a curious result, and it should be noted that as shown in this survey the income per head of London and the South-East does not exceed the national average by nearly as much as appeared from the calculations based on personal income in Chapter 6. It seems unlikely that the disparity can be entirely accounted for by differences in the definitions used; and it may be that the sample used for the expenditure survey was not large enough to give satisfactory income figures at the regional level. If the expenditure figures of this survey are compared with personal income based on the Inland Revenue figures, as was done in Table I, then London and the South-East would appear as the region with the highest propensity to save. This situation would certainly be more likely to accord with one's expectations.

An alternative approach is to compare disposable income per head and expenditure per head each expressed as a proportion of the Great

[1] This is not particularly surprising if some of the payments made for investments listed under 'other recorded items' were financed by the sale of other assets.

Britain average. This showed that the income proportion exceeded the expenditure proportion in the South and South-West and in the North Midland, Midland and Eastern group. London and the South-East, Wales and Scotland all had expenditures per head which were proportionately further above the British average than their disposable incomes. For Wales and Scotland the difference was small, but for London and the South-East it was considerable. These figures would seem to imply that the North Midland, Midland and Eastern group and the South and South-Western group have a higher propensity to save than the other regions and that substantial dissaving is probably taking place in London and the South-East. However, these results do seem rather surprising and it would be unwise to accept these as firm conclusions. It is clear that a more direct method of estimation will have to be used before satisfactory regional estimates of saving can be obtained. The figure for 'other items recorded' gives a different picture. Here London and the South-East has the highest figure followed by the South and South-West and the Midland group. Scotland has the lowest figure chiefly because of a very low outlay per head on house mortgage. It may be that this is closer to the actual pattern of savings than the results which appeared from the examination of income and expenditure. But, as explained above, some of the investments included under this heading may be financed from the sale of other investments rather than from saving out of income; the figures therefore cannot be regarded as providing satisfactory estimates of the regional propensities to save.

A comparison of these two surveys shows that over time substantial differences in the pattern of regional expenditure may occur. Moreover isolated surveys once in a while give a snapshot picture which may be affected by exceptional conditions prevailing in some of the regions at that particular time. Such conditions seemed to apply to Wales in the earlier survey. A proper study of expenditure by regions would therefore require the publication of annual estimates in the same way as one requires official estimates of gross domestic product. The Ministry of Labour are now conducting their *Family Expenditure Survey* on a regular basis and it is therefore very much to be hoped that future issues will follow the latest edition in providing regional figures. If satisfactory regional income figures could also be derived on a yearly basis one could quite easily construct integrated accounts of personal income and expenditure.

The estimation of saving seems likely to present more intractable problems. But there are few estimates which are of greater interest for regional economics. There is much less inter-connection between savings and investment in a region than there is in the nation as a whole, since a large proportion of the savings of any region are probably invested outside, and much of the investment expenditure taking place may be financed from other regions. Thus some regions may save much more than they receive in investment and others may save much less. This may be of much importance for the level of economic activity in the regions: where there is a high propensity to save and little investment taking place, purchasing power will tend to be damped down and the economy may be depressed. It is to be hoped therefore that it will eventually be possible to construct estimates which will enable this question to be properly analysed.

TABLE I
Expenditure per Head 1953–54 (Index)
United Kingdom=100

	NORTHERN	E. & W. RIDINGS	N. WESTERN	N. MIDLAND	MIDLAND	EASTERN	L. & S. EASTERN	SOUTHERN	S. WESTERN	WALES	SCOTLAND	N. IRELAND
Housing	82·1	91·5	102·5	91·3	88·9	103·0	135·2	103·5	103·7	88·9	74·5	60·5
Fuel, light	75·5	89·9	104·7	91·0	95·3	107·9	113·5	110·7	103·2	95·1	96·6	110·3
Food	95·9	99·6	100·8	99·3	101·0	97·5	105·4	93·6	95·2	102·9	96·7	86·4
Alcoholic drink	102·6	114·2	104·9	124·9	128·8	90·3	98·1	91·9	78·6	96·8	81·6	53·4
Tobacco	103·2	100·3	103·2	97·2	94·9	87·7	99·8	87·0	89·5	103·8	111·5	93·9
Clothing, etc.	84·9	132·6*	96·3	102·7	92·0	91·3	96·1	83·1	85·2	117·5	97·7	130·8
Durable Goods	102·6	110·2	101·6	116·9	104·2	84·9	105·3	89·8	75·5	123·5	73·6	74·9
Other Goods	86·0	95·8	100·0	104·9	102·2	109·6	113·5	110·4	104·9	93·9	84·9	69·5
Transport, etc.	68·0	92·2	96·0	88·6	114·2	99·1	119·0	100·0	98·1	86·2	98·3	77·1
Services	85·2	94·0	110·1	89·7	89·0	106·7	122·4	98·5	101·5	89·8	88·8	81·8
Total Expenditure	89·8	102·2	101·5	99·3	99·1	97·8	110·0	95·6	94·4	101·1	92·3	86·8
Income Tax	92·2	89·3	93·6	109·0	110·7	101·4	109·8	77·7	130·3	85·0	78·0	32·7
Nat. Insurance	95·4	100·8	103·3	99·2	102·1	98·3	97·5	94·6	99·2	102·5	99·2	97·9
Other Items Recorded†	81·2	84·9	106·8	97·0	92·4	93·1	148·4	86·7	105·6	78·7	70·2	36·7
OUTLAY (Expenditure Income Tax & National Insurance)	90·0	101·7	101·2	99·6	99·5	98·9	109·7	94·9	95·8	100·5	91·9	85·1
PERSONAL INCOME (1959/60)	86·8	98·7	98·0	97·9	108·9	87·5	127·2	98·9	80·3	83·6	87·3	63·8
Persons per household	3·29	3·05	3·17	3·18	3·28	3·14	3·04	3·24	3·10	3·15	3·28	3·84

Source: Report of an Inquiry into Household Expenditure in 1953/54, H.M.S.O., 1957.
For Personal Income see Chapter 6, Table II.

* One person in the sample spent £1,903 on one item during the period.
† Includes mortgage payments, life assurance, contributions to pensions and other insurance and to savings and holiday clubs, purchase of savings certificates. Excludes betting.

TABLE II
Expenditure per Head 1961–62 (Index)
Great Britain = 100

	NORTHERN, E.&W.RIDINGS, N.WESTERN	N.MIDLAND, MIDLAND, EASTERN	LONDON & S.EASTERN	SOUTHERN, S.WESTERN	WALES	SCOTLAND
Housing	90·2	90·3	138·3	98·7	92·3	81·0
Fuel, light & power	96·3	104·2	96·3	108·4	94·2	101·1
Food	97·7	99·2	109·2	98·9	97·1	93·2
Alcoholic drink	104·4	103·7	100·2	97·5	84·8	89·6
Tobacco	101·4	94·2	109·0	84·0	95·3	112·3
Clothing & footwear	93·5	100·6	116·0	88·3	94·2	102·5
Durable Goods	97·4	99·6	127·5	89·6	84·4	74·6
Other Goods	89·7	107·1	112·7	114·7	84·6	79·8
Transport & vehicles	89·3	107·0	121·3	98·3	90·0	80·0
Services	90·6	95·5	128·8	108·9	79·5	82·1
Total Expenditure	94·8	99·7	116·1	98·8	91·5	89·7
Income Tax	91·0	95·9	133·6	119·7	65·2	66·1
National Insurance	98·7	104·2	106·3	92·5	94·2	91·6
Other Recorded Items*	90·4	104·7	120·6	106·8	100·5	66·8
Income	94·6	102·0	114·3	101·9	88·4	86·7
Disposable Income†	94·8	102·5	112·6	100·4	90·5	88·6
Income Tax payments as % of income (G.B.=9·1)	8·8	8·6	10·6	10·7	6·7	6·9
Expenditure as % of Disposable Income	97·7	94·9	100·7	96·1	98·6	98·9

Source: *Family Expenditure Survey 1962*, H.M.S.O., 1963.

Notes: * Includes mortgage payments, life assurance, contributions to pension funds, sickness and accident insurance, contributions to Christmas, savings, or holiday clubs and purchase of savings certificates (for full details see report).

† Income less income tax and national insurance payments.

TABLE III
Expenditure per Household 1961–62 (Index)
Great Britain=100

	NORTHERN, E.&W.RIDINGS, N.WESTERN	N.MIDLAND, MIDLAND, EASTERN	LONDON & S.EASTERN	SOUTHERN, S.WESTERN	WALES	SCOTLAND
Housing	91·4	92·1	129·4	97·4	94·3	86·1
Fuel, light & power	97·6	106·3	90·2	106·9	96·4	107·5
Food	99·0	101·1	102·2	97·5	99·3	99·0
Alcoholic drink	105·7	105·5	93·6	96·1	86·7	95·2
Tobacco	102·7	96·0	102·1	82·8	97·5	119·4
Clothing & footwear	94·7	102·5	108·5	87·1	96·3	108·8
Durable Goods	98·7	101·4	119·3	88·2	86·3	79·2
Other Goods	90·8	109·2	105·6	113·1	86·5	84·7
Transport & vehicles	90·4	109·1	113·5	96·9	92·0	85·0
Services	91·7	97·4	120·6	107·4	81·3	87·2
Total Expenditure	96·0	101·6	108·7	97·4	93·6	95·3
Income Tax	92·1	97·7	125·1	118·0	66·7	70·3
National Insurance	100·1	106·4	99·6	91·3	96·5	97·3
Income	95·8	103·9	107·0	100·5	90·4	92·1
Disposable Income	96·0	104·5	105·4	99·0	92·7	94·2
Persons per household	3·04	3·06	2·81	2·96	3·07	3·19

Source: As for Table II.

CHAPTER 9

INVESTMENT IN SCOTLAND & OTHER REGIONS OF THE UNITED KINGDOM

FIGURES for investment in Scotland are unfortunately far from adequate. In fact it is impossible to get a satisfactory estimate of total investment in the Scottish economy. For certain industries, particularly transport, distribution and finance, no regional figures exist, and an attempt to produce them would raise conceptual as well as practical difficulties. With ships and airlines, for instance, it would be difficult to decide how to apportion regional estimates even if sufficiently detailed figures could be obtained. In the Welsh study estimates for these industries sometimes had to be derived by assuming the proportion of investment in the region to be the same as the region's share of the United Kingdom Gross Product.[1] This type of estimate seemed unlikely to serve a useful purpose, and it was thought better to concentrate on those sectors where reasonably reliable estimates could be derived, even if this meant that no analysis could be made of investment in the economy as a whole.

The parts of the economy which are most adequately covered are those included in the Census of Production: manufacturing industry, mining and quarrying, and gas, electricity and water. In addition to these, certain figures can be obtained for public investment in social capital: roads, houses, health, etc. A considerable amount of information on investment of this type is available from the report of the Toothill Committee, based on the submissions of Government departments.[2]

The investment figures for manufacturing industry as derived from the Censuses of Production are shown in Table I. A number of adjustments have been made to the Census figures to get comparable estimates for the whole period. The figures for Scotland and Wales

---

[1] *The Social Accounts of the Welsh Economy* (ed.), Edward Nevin, University of Wales Press.
[2] *Report of the Committee of Inquiry on the Scottish Economy* (Scottish Council), November 1961. Chapter IV.

in 1952 and 1953 are weak and should be used with caution.[1] Moreover the figures in the Census do not include new firms or establishments setting up but not yet in actual production.

It will be seen that the Scottish figure fluctuates between 7·3 and 9·3 per cent of the United Kingdom total, showing perhaps a slight tendency to fall as a proportion of the United Kingdom during periods of recession. The average for the period is 8·2 per cent. An interesting feature of this table is that the Welsh figure for investment is almost as high as the Scottish figure and in one year, 1954, is actually higher. In relation to the size of the Welsh economy the amount of investment is very high, and as will be seen this has some connection with the industrial structure of Wales.

Table II gives an index of investment at 1954 prices. It is clear from this that investment in real terms has increased substantially during the period in all the countries listed in the table. It is a characteristic of investment, however, that it fluctuates considerably from year to year. For this reason the increase as measured over an arbitrary period may be misleading if the base year happens to be good in one country and bad in another. In the period 1951–54 much the most rapid increase took place in Wales, but this was nearly all accounted for in 1954 itself. In the other countries the growth of investment took place at similar rates: the increase in the United Kingdom being somewhat faster than in Scotland and Northern Ireland. In the period 1954–60 the roles are reversed: Scotland and Northern Ireland are now the areas showing the greatest increase in investment, but for Scotland the increase is particularly marked in 1960. Over the whole period the increase is greater for Scotland, Wales and Northern Ireland than for the United Kingdom.

In Table III investment is expressed as a percentage of Gross Domestic Product arising in manufacturing industry, except for Wales where Census Net Output is used.[2] This is the gross investment ratio. This table brings out even more strongly the relative magnitude of the investment taking place in Wales during the period. The average percentage figure for Wales was 16·7 for the period 1951–58, which is much higher than that achieved by any of the other three areas and more closely comparable with the sort of investment ratios

[1] The methods used for the construction of this table are explained in the Appendix.

[2] For an explanation of the difference between Census net output and G.D.P. see Appendix, p. 155. As explained in the footnote to Table III the Welsh ratio might have been slightly higher if G.D.P. figures had been taken. For 1952 and 1953 no Welsh net output figures were available and Nevin's G.D.P. figures were used.

prevailing in West Germany. The United Kingdom investment ratio, which is customarily regarded as low by international standards, proved to be slightly higher than the Scottish or Ulster ratios, the latter being the lowest of all. Another way of putting this is that the amount of investment taking place in Scotland and Northern Ireland, was throughout the period proportionately lower than the contribution of those areas to the Gross Domestic Product of manufacturing industry in the United Kingdom. In Wales on the other hand the amount of investment was proportionately much higher than the contribution of Welsh manufacturing industry to United Kingdom Gross Domestic Product.

The industrial structure of Wales does to some extent account for the high gross investment ratio, as is shown in Table IV. In 1958 over half of all the investment in Welsh manufacturing industry took place in metal manufacture. In this industry Wales had approximately 28 per cent of the total investment for the United Kingdom and approximately four times the investment taking place in Scotland. In part this serves merely to illustrate the predominance of the steel industry in Wales, but it should be noted that, in metal manufacture investment as a proportion of net output was double the Scottish figure and substantially higher than the United Kingdom figure. It is therefore not only a matter of structure. The part of this industry which was in Wales was quite clearly investing much more than the parts in other areas of the United Kingdom.

The industries which were next in importance by amount of investment in Wales were chemicals and textiles: most probably this is accounted for mainly by oil refining and synthetic textiles. These industries also invested more as a proportion of net output in Wales than in Scotland or the United Kingdom as a whole.

The Scottish gross investment ratios by industries are much closer to those of the United Kingdom, than were those of Wales. There is a tendency, however, for the Scottish ratios to be just very slightly lower than those of the United Kingdom, and this applied to the majority of the industrial orders. There is no very marked disparity from the United Kingdom figure, as was the case for Wales, but only in chemicals, engineering and electrical, clothing, paper and printing, and other manufacturing is the Scottish ratio actually higher than that of the United Kingdom. These were all industries which played a relatively smaller part in total output of Scottish manufacturing industry than they did in the United Kingdom as a whole.[1]

The two remaining Tables, V and VI, give some details of other

[1] See Chapter 4.

SCOTLAND'S ECONOMIC PROGRESS

types of capital expenditure in Scotland. The list is necessarily incomplete for the reasons already explained, and such information as is available mostly concerns public investment. It will be noticed that in both coal and electricity, Scotland has been receiving a substantial share of United Kingdom investment, reflecting the importance of the coal industry in Scotland and the part played by hydro-electric schemes. The proportion of investment in gas, on the other hand, was small, though it leapt dramatically in 1958. Investment in the other sectors is in most cases higher than the population ratio of Scotland to the United Kingdom, the most striking case being public housing. The exceptions to this are education, where the ratio of investment was lower than the population ratio for most of the period, and private housing where the investment ratio in Scotland is remarkably low. Together with the high public investment in housing this illustrates the rather curious position of housing in Scotland.

TABLE I
Fixed Investment in Manufacturing Industry 1951–60
£ million

	SCOTLAND	WALES	N. IRELAND	UNITED KINGDOM	SCOTLAND AS % OF UNITED KINGDOM
1951	40·2	24·7	6·5	489·2	8·2
1952	38·0	24·0	6·2	502·2	7·6
1953	39·3	29·0	6·2	501·3	7·8
1954	41·2	49·8	7·0	561·3	7·3
1955	54·7	52·1	8·5	681·0	8·0
1956	75·7	47·9	9·6	830·0	9·1
1957	69·8	66·5	10·8	905·0	7·7
1958	73·4	62·0	11·5	890·0	8·2
1959	73·0	60·0	14·7	863·0	8·5
1960	96·0	91·0	15·6	1,028·0	9·3

TABLE II
Index at Constant Prices 1954=100

	SCOTLAND	WALES	N. IRELAND	UNITED KINGDOM
1951	112·4	57·0	107·1	100·4
1952	94·9	49·6	91·4	92·1
1953	95·9	58·6	88·6	89·8
1954	100·0	100·0	100·0	100·0
1955	126·0	99·2	115·7	115·2
1956	164·1	85·9	122·9	132·1
1957	144·7	113·9	131·4	137·6
1958	147·3	102·8	135·7	131·0
1959	146·8	100·0	174·3	127·6
1960	191·7	150·2	182·9	150·7
% increase 1951–60	170·5	263·5	170·7	150·3

For Sources and Methods, see Appendix.

TABLE III
Investment as a Percentage of Gross Domestic Product in Manufacturing 1951–60

	SCOTLAND	WALES*	N. IRELAND*	UNITED KINGDOM
1951	8·9	13·4	8·7	9·9
1952	8·3	12·2	9·4	10·1
1953	8·0	15·1	8·0	9·3
1954	7·7	19·3	8·0	9·5
1955	9·7	17·8	9·3	10·4
1956	12·5	15·6	9·7	12·1
1957	10·8	20·5	10·4	12·4
1958	10·8	20·0	10·9	12·0
1959	10·7	—	12·7	10·9
1960	13·0	—	12·2	12·0
Average† 1951–60	10·0	—	9·9	10·9
Average† 1951–58	9·6	16·7	9·3	10·7

Note: *Northern Ireland figures were derived using estimates for the contribution of manufacturing industry to G.D.P. obtained from the Economic Advisory Office of the Northern Ireland Government. Welsh figures are expressed as a percentage of Census 'net output' except for 1952 and 1953 when Nevin's figures of G.D.P. in manufacturing are used. Owing to the difference in definition, net output is slightly larger than the contribution to G.D.P. (see Appendix, p. 155). The percentage figures for Wales might therefore have been slightly higher if G.D.P. figures had been used for all years.

†This is an unweighted average of the investment ratios in each year. It has been suggested that this is not the best sort of average to take and that a better method might have been to express the total investment for the period as a percentage of manufacturing G.D.P. for all years. However, owing to the effect of inflation, this would tend to give undue weight to the position prevailing in the later years. Undoubtedly the best method would have been to take total investment as a percentage of G.D.P. using constant prices throughout. But the figures at constant prices are not entirely satisfactory owing to the inadequacy of the price data; and it was therefore felt that such a method would only provide an additional source of error.

TABLE IV
Fixed Investment in Manufacturing 1958 by Industries

	AS % OF NET OUTPUT			£ million		
	SCOTLAND	WALES	U.K.	SCOTLAND	WALES	U.K.
Bricks, Pottery, Cement, etc.	10·6	13·2	11·5	2·1	1·4	34·1
Chemicals & Allied	26·3	32·8	22·2	13·4	11·9	208·6
Metal Manufacture	14·4	30·7	19·8	9·5	37·7	136·2
Engineering & Electrical	11·0	2·9	8·0	15·5	1·0	139·5
Shipbuilding & Marine Engineering	10·1	—	10·7	5·3 ⎫	1·4	21·7
Vehicles	5·8	—	7·8	1·0 ⎭		63·4
Metal Goods	5·7	7·1	7·1	1·3	1·3	31·2
Textiles	6·6	13·3	8·1	4·3	3·2	49·7
Leather	3·4	7·1	3·7	0·1	0·1	1·6
Clothing	3·5	3·5	2·7	0·5	0·2	8·3
Food, Drink & Tobacco	10·2	8·8	10·7	11·2	1·5	98·0
Timber	4·4	11·6	5·0	0·7	0·5	10·6
Paper, Printing & Publishing	10·7	13·4	10·6	5·3	1·1	61·2
Other Manufacturing	15·1	6·9	11·4	2·1	0·7	25·8
Total	11·0	20·0	11·3	72·4	62·0	890·0

Note: Some of the totals differ slightly from the 1958 figures given in Table I, since the latter are adjusted to compare with 1954 (Appendix, p. 176).

Source: Census of Production 1958.

TABLE V
Other Capital Expenditure
£ million

	1951	1954	1955	1956	1957	1958	1959	1960
Coal Mines	3·3	8·4	11·7	15·1	15·6	15·3	16·9	11·7
Gas	2·4	3·8	4·0	3·4	2·7	2·8	6·1	5·5
Electricity	20·9	32·0	36·4	36·5	35·5	42·5	40·7	35·3
Water Services	—	5·1	5·3	5·0	3·8	3·5	4·2	5·7
Roads & Lighting	—	2·2	2·6	3·4	4·6	5·5	9·0	13·5
Housing Public	—	60·1	50·3	50·9	51·9	45·0	40·7	41·1
Housing Private	—	5·5	7·6	10·1	7·9	9·0	11·1	17·0
Education	—	6·8	8·8	10·7	12·4	13·1	15·0	15·7
Health	—	3·9	4·0	4·0	4·2	3·8	4·4	5·2

TABLE VI
As a Percentage of U.K.

	1951	1954	1955	1956	1957	1958	1959	1960
Coal Mines	11·9	11·9	15·1	18·5	17·2	14·7	15·1	13·7
Gas	6·0	7·2	6·9	6·7	5·2	5·6	13·9	13·1
Electricity	14·0	14·6	14·5	14·6	13·3	14·3	12·0	10·3
Water Services	—	14·2	14·7	12·2	9·3	8·3	11·4	13·3
Roads & Lighting	—	12·9	11·3	10·3	11·8	8·9	11·1	16·3
Housing Public	—	14·3	14·2	15·1	16·5	16·7	15·4	15·0
Housing Private	—	2·4	2·9	3·4	2·6	2·8	2·8	3·5
Education	—	8·3	9·8	9·5	9·2	9·4	10·4	10·7
Health	—	15·6	14·8	14·3	12·7	10·6	10·7	11·6

Sources: Coal, Gas and Electricity 1951–8, *Census of Production*. Remaining figures from *Report of the Committee of Inquiry into the Scottish Economy*. Scottish Council, pp. 45–47.

Census figures are not exactly comparable with the remainder.

CHAPTER 10

INVESTMENT AND GROWTH

IN recent years there has been much discussion of the United Kingdom's slow economic growth and of the importance of investment as a factor contributing towards this. This is a subject of much controversy and there are those who argue that the attempt to explain Britain's slow rate of growth in terms of the rather low investment ratio is a serious oversimplification.[1] Despite this it remains a fact that Britain's poor economic growth has been associated with a ratio of investment as a proportion of Gross National Product which is low, measured either gross or net. Dr Lamfalussy's recent study has shed much new light on this question and drawn a number of comparisons which seem to support the view that investment plays an important role.[2] Whatever the verdict, it is an inescapable conclusion that the more rapid rate of growth of one country as compared with another must be associated either with higher investment or with a more favourable marginal capital/output ratio, which would indicate that for a given investment the return in terms of increased output is greater.

The application of this type of analysis to the regions of the United Kingdom has not hitherto been attempted, but it was thought that it might yield some interesting results.[3] Owing to the inadequate information on investment by regions, it is not possible to apply this analysis to the growth of Gross Domestic Product as a whole; but it can be applied fairly satisfactorily to manufacturing industry, and this compares quite well with Lamfalussy's analysis of growth and investment in British, German and Italian manufacturing industry.[4]

The first step is to relate the gross investment ratio to the rate of

---

[1] See for instance, A. K. Cairncross, *Factors in Economic Development*, Chapters 5 and 9. Allen & Unwin, 1962.

[2] Alexandre Lamfalussy, *The United Kingdom and the Six*. Macmillan, 1963.

[3] In the following section I have borrowed extensively from the techniques used by Lamfalussy, whose book to a great extent inspired this analysis.

[4] Op. cit., Chapter VII.

growth. The gross investment ratios used are simply the average over the period of the yearly gross investment ratios given in Table III of the last chapter.[1] Growth is taken as measured by the indices of industrial production in manufacturing industry for Scotland, Wales and Northern Ireland; the United Kingdom figure is gross domestic product in manufacturing industry at constant prices.[2]

This is not entirely satisfactory. Unlike the other areas Wales has no official index and the figures constructed by Professor Beacham and Dr Nevin do not go beyond 1958; moreover they are for the whole of Welsh industry, not just manufacturing. It was decided therefore to use Dr Nevin's earlier index for manufacturing industry from the *Social Accounts of the Welsh Economy*; this gives 1951–56 and the last two years were obtained by assuming that manufacturing industry expanded at the same rate as industry as a whole shown in the later Beacham–Nevin index. Since the indices for industry as a whole move very closely with manufacturing industry in the earlier period it seems unlikely that this procedure will introduce much error. The Welsh case was obviously very interesting, and it would therefore have been a pity to exclude it from the analysis. But owing to the lack of data the Welsh analysis had to be confined to the period 1951–58. As will be seen 1958 was not a good year to take as the end of the period, since the whole British economy was in something of a recession at that time; and with 1951 a boom year, measurements of growth may seriously underestimate the growth of capacity. It was impossible to get round this difficulty if Wales was to be included in the analysis; but, because of this, figures were also calculated for the other three areas up to 1960.

The Scottish and Irish indices are official indices which are kept regularly up to date. They should therefore be more reliable and easier to handle than the Welsh figures. However, the extraordinarily small growth registered by the Scottish figures did give rise to some suspicion especially over the period 1954–58. This has already been discussed at some length in Chapter 5 where it was shown that the index over this period is only compatible with growth at current prices measured by the 1954 and 1958 Census of Production, if the output of Scottish manufacturing industry experienced a more rapid

---

[1] See the footnote to Table III (Chapter 9).

[2] *Digest of Scottish Statistics, Census of Production for Northern Ireland, 1958, National Income and Expenditure 1962*, H.M.S.O. Welsh figures from *The Social Accounts of the Welsh Economy 1948–56* and A. Beacham and E. T. Nevin, *The Welsh Economy 1960*, London and Cambridge Economic Bulletin, December 1960, Appendix, Table I.

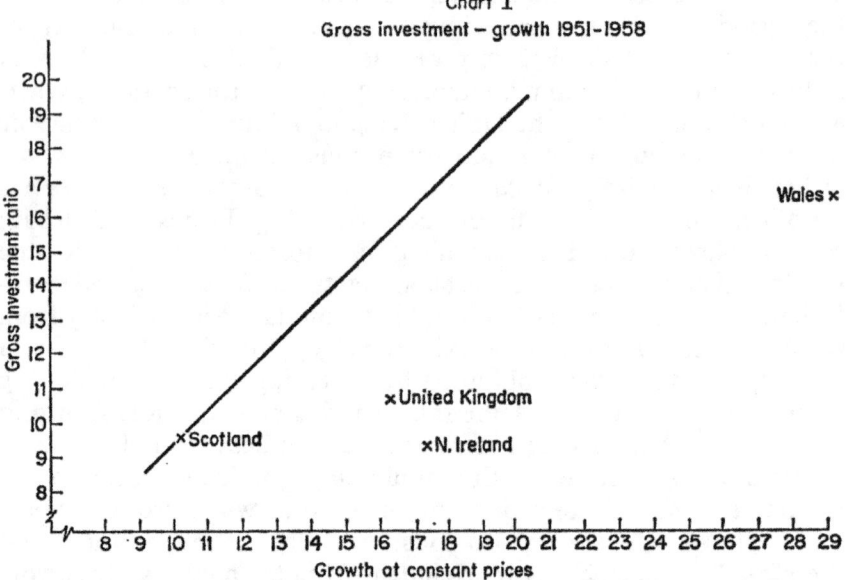

Chart I
Gross investment — growth 1951-1958

price rise than that of United Kingdom manufacturing output as a whole.[1] It may be reasonable that the prices of Scottish output should rise more rapidly than those of the United Kingdom; but if it is not, or if the rates of price increase shown in Chapter 5 are unrealistic, then the Scottish index of industrial production must of necessity underestimate Scottish growth. It was decided to proceed with the analysis using the official Scottish index, since there was no alternative; but throughout the analysis it must be borne in mind that it may possibly underestimate Scottish growth.

Rather the reverse situation applied to the Northern Irish index. The growth shown by this index was only compatible with growth at current prices if Irish output experienced a smaller rise in price than that of the United Kingdom over the period 1951-58. As explained in Chapter 5 this seemed more readily explicable intuitively than the divergence between Scottish and United Kingdom prices.

The relationship between gross investment and economic growth 1951-58 is illustrated in Chart I. It will be seen that the United Kingdom and Wales, both of whom have higher gross investment ratios than Scotland also have a more rapid rate of economic growth. The difference in the case of Wales is very large indeed. Northern Ireland on the other hand has the lowest gross investment ratio of all and yet achieves a growth rate as rapid as that of the United King-

[1] See pp. 63-65.

dom. Apart from the Irish case, therefore, there seems *prima facie* to be some sort of association between higher investment and a more rapid rate of growth.

The important question is whether Scotland, by raising her investment to the United Kingdom or Welsh level could attain similar rates of economic growth. Table I shows that, in the circumstances depicted in the chart, Scotland has a very much higher gross marginal capital output/ratio than the other areas. *If this had to be maintained*, Scottish investment at the Welsh level would yield approximately 18 per cent growth, not greatly exceeding the United Kingdom rate, and very far behind the growth of 29 per cent which Wales actually achieved.

The figures for 1951–60 in Table I show the effect on the gross marginal capital/output ratio of taking the longer period. In fact all the ratios fall substantially. This is accounted for by the fact that 1958 was a year of recession while 1960 was one of comparative boom. Even on the basis of these figures, however, if Scotland was to maintain the same capital/output ratio the investment ratio would have to rise to 17 per cent if Scotland was to achieve even the United Kingdom rate of growth.

TABLE I

	GROSS INVESTMENT RATIO	RATE OF GROWTH (YEARLY)	GROSS MARGINAL CAPITAL/ OUTPUT RATIO
	1951–58		
Scotland[1]	9·6	1·3	7·4
Wales	16·7	3·7	4·5
N. Ireland	9·3	2·3	4·0
United Kingdom	10·7	2·2	4·9
	1951–60		
Scotland	10·0	1·9	5·3
N. Ireland	9·9	3·0	3·3
United Kingdom	10·9	3·2	3·4

The figures for both periods show Scotland to have a less favourable gross marginal capital/output ratio than the other areas. Northern Ireland appears to be most favourably placed with the United Kingdom and Wales holding an intermediate position. If investment could be related to output capacity instead of actual output, the Scottish ratio might well be more favourable. Scotland suffered more severely from the recession of 1958 than the United Kingdom as a whole and did not benefit so much from the subse-

[1] Scotland's position is much improved by using the revised index of industrial production (see p. 136). This gives a rate of growth of 2·0 and a gross marginal capital/output ratio of 4·8. 1960 figures were not finalized.

quent boom.[1] The difference between actual and potential output was therefore probably greater in Scotland than it was in the United Kingdom both in 1958 and 1960. In 1951 on the other hand both Scotland and the United Kingdom were experiencing boom conditions from the Korean War and the difference between actual and potential output was probably small in both areas. If these qualifications are taken into account, the Scottish position must be somewhat more favourable than at first appears.

But even ignoring these qualifications, it is misleading to assume that the gross marginal capital/output ratio would in itself remain independent of the rate of growth, as was done in the analysis above. Such an assumption implies that replacement forms the same proportion of gross investment regardless of the rate of growth. The significance of this must now be examined.

A large part of gross investment is, of course, replacement of existing capital equipment. This is required to maintain the capital stock and keep output at its existing level. It is only net investment or investment over and above replacement which can properly claim to have any connection with the rate of growth. If one could assume that net investment always moved in proportion to gross investment, this qualification would not matter but this is far from being the case. Clearly, a country with no economic growth and no growth in productivity per man employed would require no net investment to maintain a constant level of output, and all investment could be regarded as replacement. At the other extreme, one would expect a country with a very rapid rate of growth to spend a large part of its investment on equipment other than replacement. The ratio of net to gross investment would therefore be high. The proportion of investment which goes into new equipment other than replacement therefore varies with the rate of growth.

In practice it is often extremely difficult to make a clear distinction between net and gross investment. Much investment which replaces existing capital equipment takes the form of substituting an improved version of the plant which was replaced. It may be capable of a greater output, or of higher output per man, and therefore contains an element of net investment; but it is often extremely difficult in such cases, even for those who install the plant, to estimate what proportion of this gross investment expenditure is strictly replacement and what is net investment.

Yet in analysing the connection between investment and economic growth this distinction is of the first importance; and to get an

[1] This is shown by the figures for Gross Domestic Product in Chapter 2.

INVESTMENT AND GROWTH

accurate picture of the productivity of investment, it is therefore not adequate to compare economic growth with the gross investment ratio. The only relevant comparison is between economic growth and the net investment ratio. In a country with a low rate of growth, therefore, a comparison of growth with the gross investment ratio is always inclined to make investment look unproductive, since this ratio conceals the fact that in such a country net investment is likely to account for an unusually small proportion of total investment, the bulk of it being spent on replacement. To some extent this must explain the high gross marginal capital/output ratio for Scotland.

To assess the importance of this, and to calculate the true productivity of investment net investment ratios have to be used. The difficulty with this is that reliable net investment figures are hard to obtain for most countries, and are totally absent for Scotland, Wales and Northern Ireland. Fortunately, it is possible to follow Lamfalussy's technique and derive net investment from the other variables. Since the proportion that net investment forms of gross investment varies according to the rate of growth of output, it is possible to derive a figure for the net investment ratio, if the gross investment ratio and the rate of growth and the time cycle of replacement are all known. The present study follows Dr Lamfalussy in assuming the time cycle for replacement to be twenty years in manufacturing industry. The actual formula used by Lamfalussy is:[1]

$$a = \frac{1 - \frac{1}{(1+g)^t}}{\frac{1}{aG} - \frac{1}{(1+g)^t}}$$

where a = the net investment ratio.
  aG = the gross investment ratio.
  g = the yearly rate of growth.
  t = the time period.

A feature of this method is that it carries the implicit assumption that all capital equipment falling due for replacement is actually replaced. Net investment is taken as the surplus after all replacement needs have been met.[2] In practice any economy is constantly changing its structure, and those industries which are in decline may not have all their capital equipment replaced as it falls due. Instead the capital

[1] Dr Lamfalussy's technique is given in detail in his book (op. cit.). Appendix II.
[2] This is common to most definitions of net investment. Net investment is the *increase* in the stock of capital regardless of any changes in composition.

equipment of some industries may actually contract while new investment is taking place in other sectors of the economy. The method used here cannot take account of this.

The results of the calculations using this formula for the areas concerned with this analysis are shown in Table II.

TABLE II

	NET INVESTMENT RATIO	YEARLY RATE OF GROWTH	NET MARGINAL CAPITAL/ OUTPUT RATIO
1951–58			
Scotland[1]	2·4	1·3	1·8
Wales	9·4	3·7	2·5
N. Ireland	3·3	2·3	1·4
United Kingdom	4·1	2·2	1·9
1951–60			
Scotland	4·1	1·9	2·2
N. Ireland	4·7	3·0	1·6
United Kingdom	5·4	3·2	1·7

The Scottish net investment ratio, especially over the period 1951–58 is remarkably low at only 2·4 per cent; and only the Welsh ratio comes near to the sort of level commonly found to prevail in continental countries. Precisely because it is so low, however, Scottish investment when measured net appeared to be much more productive in terms of output than gross investment was. As measured by the net marginal capital/output ratio, Scottish investment in the period 1951–58 is actually slightly more productive in terms of growth than United Kingdom investment, though the difference is so small as to be of no significance and the position is reversed if the period 1951 to 1960 is taken. Northern Ireland remains in the most favourable position, though its marginal capital/output ratio is very close to the United Kingdom for 1951–60, and Wales now has the worst net marginal capital/output ratio.

The results are illustrated in Chart II. It will be seen that the chart comes out very much better using net investment than gross. This is partly because of the change in the relative position of Scotland and Northern Ireland: the latter's faster growth now being associated with a higher investment ratio instead of a slightly lower one. Northern Ireland is still more favourably placed than Scotland, but

[1] The revised index of industrial production gives a net investment ratio of 3·4, a rate of growth of 2·0 and a net marginal capital/output ratio of 1·7.

INVESTMENT AND GROWTH

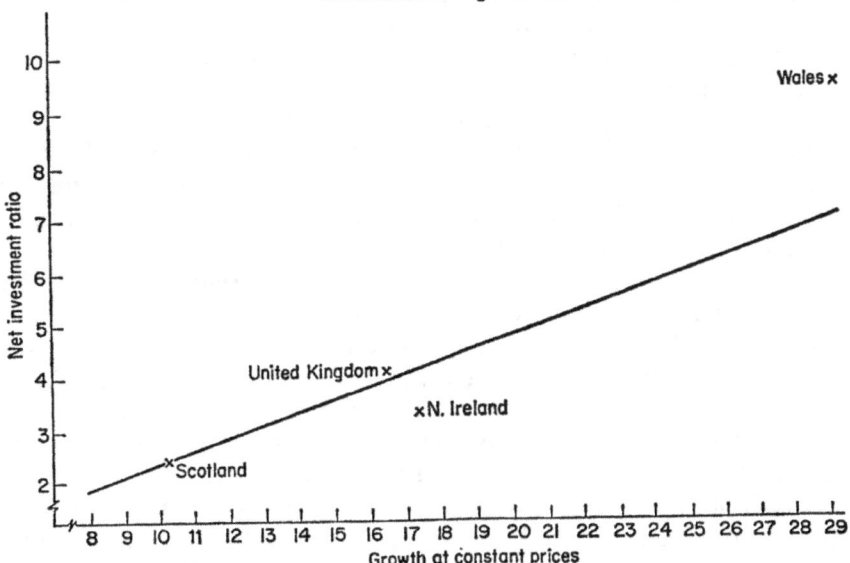

Chart II
Net investment – growth 1951–1958

the difference is no longer quite so extraordinary. The other main change is that the marginal capital/output ratios are now much closer than when gross investment was used. A line is drawn on the chart representing the Scottish net marginal capital/output ratio: for any investment ratio this shows the corresponding rate of growth. From this it can be seen how the productivity of Scottish investment in terms of growth compares with the other areas. As with the figures in Table II Scotland and the United Kingdom are about equally placed. Wales is less favourable; Northern Ireland more favourable.

It is still not legitimate to deduce from this that if Scotland had enjoyed the Welsh net investment ratio she would have achieved even more growth than Wales.[1] Apart from the points made earlier about actual output and potential output, it must be remembered that these calculations only refer to *marginal* capital/output ratios. There is no reason for the ratios to remain the same for any level of growth or investment. As investment expands it may be subject to either diminishing or increasing returns in terms of the growth of output which results; and there is therefore no means of telling how Scotland would do given the Welsh or United Kingdom levels of investment.

[1] It would appear that Dr Lamfalussy is inclined to fall into this error in making his European comparisons (op. cit.).

The chart does not purport to show this. But the line representing a fixed marginal capital/output ratio does illustrate the effect of a marginal increment in investment in each of the regions. It is clear that in the period 1951–58 the marginal productivity of investment in terms of growth of output was highest in Northern Ireland, lowest in Wales, with Scotland and the United Kingdom taking an intermediate position. Any marginal increase in investment provided that it was representative of that already taking place, would therefore seem likely to yield a better growth if devoted to Northern Ireland or Scotland rather than to Wales.

However, the particular years taken are of great importance to this type of analysis. This may be seen at a glance if the United Kingdom figures derived for 1951–60 in this study are compared with Lamfalussy's figures for 1953–60. Lamfalussy finds the United Kingdom to have a net investment ratio of 5·9 instead of our 5·4, a growth rate of 3·8 per cent per annum, and a net marginal capital/output ratio of 1·5 compared with our 1·7.

It is difficult to assess how a different time period would affect this study. If the period 1954–58 is taken, Wales and Scotland both come out worse than over the longer period. Although Wales maintains her high level of investment, her growth is no better than that of the U.K. during this time. Scottish growth over the same period amounts to a mere 2 per cent. Clearly, such a period is too short to give meaningful results and one cannot deduce from them that in Scotland and Wales replacement formed a higher proportion of total investment during these years, or that the capital/output ratio deteriorated. Most probably this is a good instance of a period when the actual growth of output fell very far short of the growth of capacity or potential output.

Over a longer period such problems tend to assume rather less importance, and it is interesting that the figures in Table II for 1951–60 largely confirm the pattern of 1951–58. Investment ratios and rates of growth are both somewhat higher owing to the recovery of the economy and the increase in investment in 1959 and 1960. But the marginal capital/output ratios remain similar, rising slightly for Scotland and Northern Ireland, owing to a particularly sharp increase in investment, and falling for the United Kingdom as a result of the more rapid growth. The position of Scotland and the United Kingdom is therefore reversed in that the United Kingdom has the more favourable marginal capital/output ratio over this period.

There remains one further aspect of investment and growth to be discussed. This is the relationship between investment and the in-

INVESTMENT AND GROWTH

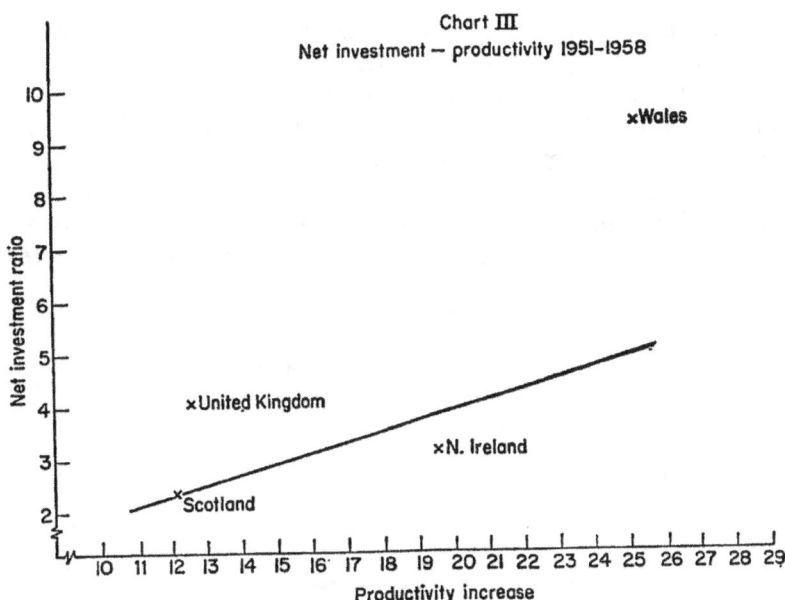

Chart III
Net investment — productivity 1951–1958

crease in productivity. Employment in manufacturing industry has risen in some areas of the United Kingdom and fallen in others, so that the relationship between investment and increased productivity may be quite different from that between investment and growth. Unfortunately, as in so many other cases, the statistics are far from adequate. It is impossible to get figures for regions in man-years; all one can do is to derive output per person employed of total employment in manufacturing industry as given in the Censuses of Production. This can be done for the period 1951–58 and adjustment to constant prices can be made by using the indices of industrial production. No adjustment for part-time employment can be made, and it can only be assumed that the effect of this between regions cancels out.

Employment fluctuates a certain amount in all regions, but the net effect over the whole period seems to be that Scottish and Northern Irish employment in manufacturing industry both fall by approximately 2 per cent; Welsh employment rises by 3 per cent and United Kingdom employment goes up by 4 per cent. When this is applied to get the growth of output per head at constant prices, it is found that Scotland and the United Kingdom both have an increase in productivity of 12 per cent over the period 1951–58; Northern Ireland has an increase of 19 per cent; and Wales an increase of 25 per cent. In Scotland and Northern Ireland, therefore, the growth in productivity per head exceeds the rate of growth of output as a whole, while in England and Wales the reverse is the case.

Chart III shows the effect of relating this to net investment. The result is substantially different from that which appeared in the comparison of investment and growth. Northern Ireland once again appears to get the best return from investment; but in relation to the amount of investment, Scotland achieves a bigger increase in productivity than the United Kingdom. Wales achieves a smaller increase.

TABLE III

	NET INVESTMENT RATIO	GROWTH OF PRODUCTIVITY (YEARLY)	NET MARGINAL INVESTMENT/ PRODUCTIVITY RATIO
Scotland[1]	2·4	1·7	1·4
Wales	9·4	3·3	2·8
Northern Ireland	3·1	2·5	1·2
United Kingdom	4·1	1·7	2·4

CONCLUSION

The main conclusion which emerges from this study is that the return on investment in Scotland in terms of economic growth in manufacturing industry was about the same as in the United Kingdom, not as good as in Northern Ireland, but slightly better than in Wales. On the other hand, the return in terms of increased productivity was again best in Northern Ireland, but it was substantially better in Scotland than in the United Kingdom and Wales.

What this means is that a greater proportion of net investment in Scotland and Northern Ireland has been devoted to capital deepening than in the United Kingdom, and a smaller proportion to capital widening. In simpler terms, proportionately more has been spent on producing the same output with less labour, and rather less on expanding output which would involve the employment of more labour. It is perhaps unfortunate that this should have been so at a time when both Scotland and Northern Ireland were experiencing unemployment which was above the national average. In such circumstances one would prefer to see the emphasis placed on expansion of output rather than increased output per person employed. It is regions such as the Midlands or London and the South-East, which suffer from labour shortages, that have a particular need for increased productivity if their economic growth is not to be impeded.

[1] The revised index gives a net investment ratio of 3·4 and a growth of productivity of 2·4. The investment/productivity ratio is unaltered (see p. 136).

INVESTMENT AND GROWTH

Ironical though the situation may seem, however, it is not altogether surprising. Scotland and Northern Ireland are both regions in need of structural readjustment and where traditional industries face a stagnant market combined with keen competition from overseas. Such industries in order to survive are compelled to invest heavily in labour-saving equipment so that their costs can be kept down. But the best they can hope for is to retain their share of the market; an expansion of output is not expected or planned for. This situation would seem to fit the experience of the shipbuilding industry in recent years; and it may well apply also to other traditional industries of the Scottish and Northern Irish economies, such as textiles, locomotive manufacture and certain types of engineering.[1]

In Northern Ireland's case there is the additional factor that output per head in manufacturing industry is far below the United Kingdom level, even with the more rapid rate of productivity increase.[2] The scope for raising productivity is therefore very high in this region, and any new investment whether in existing industries or new industries might be expected to show a high return in terms of increased productivity. Existing industry is clearly more labour intensive than in the rest of the United Kingdom; but it is unlikely that new investment would be planned to achieve different degrees of capital and labour intensity even if the level of earnings is lower in some regions than others. To this extent, therefore, Northern Ireland's higher rate of productivity increase may be partly caused by her need to catch up with the rest of the United Kingdom.

One thing which is abundantly clear from this study is that the amount of investment taking place in both Scotland and Northern Ireland was inadequate in the period 1951–60. It is desirable that both of these regions should eventually be able to equal the United Kingdom as a whole in their standards of living and general economic performance. In this respect, Northern Ireland failed to narrow the gap significantly, and Scotland fell further behind during the period. Both regions had a lower investment ratio, however measured, than the United Kingdom; yet the return on investment in terms of growth seemed to be as good as, and in the Northern Irish case better than the United Kingdom. It is clear from this that the investment ratio in these two regions needs to be stepped up substantially. There is no reason to suppose that increased investment here would

[1] This situation is very close to that described by Dr Lamfalussy in his book on the Belgian economy, see *Investment and Growth in Mature Economies: the case of Belgium*. Macmillan, 1961.
[2] See Chapter 4, Table IV.

be less productive than elsewhere in the United Kingdom. And if Scotland and Northern Ireland are to catch up with the United Kingdom in economic performance, they may well need investment ratios which are above the United Kingdom level.

CHAPTER 11

SUMMARY OF THE MAIN FINDINGS AND THE NEED FOR FURTHER IMPROVEMENT IN REGIONAL STATISTICS

SUMMARY OF THE MAIN FINDINGS

THE aim of this book was to analyse certain aspects of the Scottish economy in greater detail than has been attempted before. It may be said that the results confirm, for the most part, the impression which most people already have. Scotland is customarily thought of as lagging behind the United Kingdom economy in the 1950s; to demonstrate that this was so will not be considered very original. But what this book tries to do is to provide a factual basis for what was mainly an impression before, and to measure in quantifiable terms the extent to which the Scottish economy is lagging behind the United Kingdom. Though many people thought Scotland had a poorer rate of economic growth and a lower level of income per head than the United Kingdom, few people could say how much poorer the rate of growth was or how much lower the level of income per head. In quantifying these differences one is able to assess not only the extent of the improvement which would be required to put the Scottish economy on a par with the United Kingdom, but also the relative position of Scotland and some of the other standard regions of the United Kingdom.

The central part of this analysis is the estimate of Gross Domestic Product. This is the measure of the output of goods and services produced in the region. Without this it is impossible to assess the share of United Kingdom output contributed by Scotland, to compare rates of growth of output in Scotland and the United Kingdom or to contrast levels of output per head in Scotland and the United Kingdom. Comparisons of rates of growth have sometimes been made in the past by comparing the official indices of industrial production for Scotland and the United Kingdom; but this does not provide a satisfactory guide to the performance of the economy as a whole, since the index covers only manufacturing industry, mining, gas, electricity and water, and construction. These industries account for little more than 40 per cent of Gross Domestic Product.

SCOTLAND'S ECONOMIC PROGRESS

The estimates presented in this book show that Scottish Gross Domestic Product as a proportion of the United Kingdom total fell from 9·3 per cent in 1951 to 8·7 per cent in 1960; gross domestic product per head fell from 92 per cent of the United Kingdom level to 88 per cent. The rate of growth of gross domestic product at constant prices was similar in Scotland and the United Kingdom between 1951 and 1954; but between 1954 and 1960 Scottish growth was only 9 per cent compared with 18 per cent for the United Kingdom.[1] There is thus a clear and unmistakable tendency for Scotland to lag behind the United Kingdom; but in the years for which comparison was possible gross domestic product per head was higher in Scotland than in Wales or Northern Ireland. The difference between Scotland and Wales in this respect was very small, but with Northern Ireland it was substantial.

Figures for output per head of occupied population by industries shows that Scottish productivity was furthest behind the United Kingdom in mining, distribution and construction, where the difference ranged from 14 to 20 per cent. Productivity in manufacturing was only 4 per cent below the United Kingdom average; in agriculture, forestry and fishing it was virtually the same; and in gas, electricity and water it was slightly higher in Scotland.

Income from employment in Scotland rose 66 per cent between 1951 and 1960 compared with 78 per cent for the United Kingdom. The bulk of this difference, however, arises because employment has expanded less in Scotland than in the rest of the United Kingdom. Income per employee in Scotland was 95 per cent of the United Kingdom level in 1951 compared with 93 per cent in 1960. Moreover, income per employee at current prices rose 65 per cent in Scotland from 1951 to 1960 as against 67 per cent in the United Kingdom. Scottish income per employee is therefore not so very far behind the United Kingdom level even now, especially if the effect of high earnings in London and the South-East on the United Kingdom figure is considered; and income per employee has risen almost as fast as in the United Kingdom despite the much poorer economic growth of the Scottish economy.

Gross profits, income from self-employment and other trading income rose more slowly in Scotland during the period than in the United Kingdom. As a proportion of the United Kingdom total, Scottish income from self-employment and gross profits of companies both fell. On the other hand profits and self-employment income seemed to form a larger part of Scottish gross domestic pro-

[1] The revised index may raise the Scottish figure to about 10% (see p. 136).

SUMMARY OF THE MAIN FINDINGS

duct in a number of industries than in the United Kingdom. This may be connected with the particular structure of Scottish business and may indeed be the counterpart of a lower salary income.

The analysis of the output of manufacturing industry showed that food, drink and tobacco, metal manufacture, shipbuilding and marine engineering, textiles, and paper, printing and publishing played a proportionately larger part in Scotland than in the United Kingdom. Chemicals and vehicles were the most seriously underrepresented. Analysed at the level of order groups, however, it was clear that the Scottish economy was much closer in character to the United Kingdom than either Wales, with its heavy specialization in metal manufacture, or Northern Ireland, which is heavily weighted by food, drink and tobacco, and textiles. The evidence therefore suggested that the most important structural differences between the Scottish and United Kingdom economies are within order groups. Obvious examples of this would seem to be provided by vehicles and metal manufacture.

The index of industrial production gives Scotland a much lower rate of growth for manufacturing output than the United Kingdom. Scottish growth between 1954 and 1960 was only 9 per cent compared with 23 per cent for the United Kingdom and 18 per cent for Northern Ireland.[1] Moreover the only industries for which Scottish growth exceeded the U.K. rate were engineering and electrical, textiles, and clothing. The traditional view that Scotland's low rate of growth was due to a structural bias in favour of older declining and slower growing industries, seemed difficult to uphold when the poor rate of growth was to be seen in every order group except three.

Scotland's output per person employed in manufacturing industry was higher than Northern Ireland, but not as high as Wales or the United Kingdom. In Northern Ireland output per person employed was below the United Kingdom average for almost every industry, the most notable case being textiles. Wales had an extremely high output per person employed in metal manufacture and textiles. Scotland's output per head was above the United Kingdom level in food, drink and tobacco, engineering and electrical industries, leather and leather goods, and bricks, pottery and glass.

The study of prices showed that the prices of manufacturing output in Scotland has risen faster than in the United Kingdom since 1954, while in Northern Ireland they had risen more slowly since 1951. The Scottish estimates by orders, however, cast some doubt on the growth figures shown in the Scottish index of industrial production.

[1] Revised index will probably give a Scottish figure of about 14 per cent.

The analysis of personal income in the standard regions of the United Kingdom showed that Scotland's income per head of total population was 87 per cent of the United Kingdom level. It was above the level in Northern Ireland, the South-West or Wales. London and the South-East had by far the highest income per head, and since this region accounted for 27 per cent of the total for all regions, the United Kingdom average was greatly influenced by it. Property income played a remarkably small part in Scotland compared with other regions, but investment income as a whole was higher in Scotland, per head of total population, than in most of the other regions.

Within Scotland the Clydeside region had a higher income per head than either of the other two main regions, the North or the South. This region had a lower investment income but a higher earned income than either of the others. Figures for income by counties showed West Lothian to have the lowest income per head followed by the northern highland group. Excluding Renfrew which was taken together with the other counties of the Clydeside conurbation, Midlothian had the highest income per head. Dunbarton, Renfrew and Lanark taken together had an income per head above the Scottish average and in absolute terms, they accounted for 43 per cent of the Scottish total. This illustrates the remarkable extent to which the Clydeside conurbation dominates the Scottish economy. Its role is even more important than the part played by London and the South-East region in the United Kingdom economy.

The survey of consumers' expenditure showed that Scotland had a very low expenditure per head on housing, alcoholic drink and durable goods, but that expenditure on tobacco was the highest of any region. Income tax payments per head were well below the national average. Unfortunately it proved very difficult to relate the expenditure figures to income in a satisfactory manner; and it was impossible therefore to derive reliable estimates of the propensity to save.

The section on investment showed that both Scotland and Northern Ireland had somewhat lower ratios of investment to gross domestic product in manufacturing industry than the United Kingdom. The significance of this becomes more apparent when one remembers that the United Kingdom ratio is normally considered to be very low by international standards. The Welsh ratio, on the other hand, was high and in a different category from the United Kingdom and the other two regions.

The attempt to relate the investment ratios to the rates of economic growth achieved in manufacturing industry showed that Scotland's growth in relation to gross investment was very poor. But if a net

SUMMARY OF THE MAIN FINDINGS

investment ratio is used, the relationship between growth and investment is much better, the Scottish results being similar to those for the United Kingdom, though not quite as good as Northern Ireland's. There was evidence that both Scottish and Northern Irish investment had been directed more towards raising productivity per person employed than United Kingdom investment. This seemed paradoxical in regions with fairly high unemployment, but was understandable in terms of the modernization programmes in traditional industries. Unfortunately the analysis of investment and rates of growth was made much less satisfactory than it ought to be by the inadequacy of important statistics and the likelihood of errors arising in the indices of industrial production, which were used to measure economic growth. Until these are improved the results must be regarded as tentative and the conclusions accepted with caution.

THE NEED FOR FURTHER IMPROVEMENT IN REGIONAL STATISTICS

The estimates presented in this book cover only some of the basic economic statistics required to make a serious economic study of a region. Many other measurements are required, some no less important than those given here, if regional policy is to be properly directed. But at present it seemed impossible to go beyond what has been attempted here simply because the basic material on which the estimates must be based is inadequate or is not available. However, it is to be hoped, and indeed expected, that a better flow of information on regions will gradually be made available by government departments. In time, therefore, it may be possible to obtain better estimates for the main economic variables on a regional basis. Adequate changes are perhaps unlikely, for nothing short of a complete revolution in the provision of regional statistics could be considered satisfactory.

At this stage it is perhaps useful to consider the main improvements which need to be made and their relevance to the formulation of regional policy. Under the present arrangement figures for insured employees and unemployment are almost the only statistics for all the standard regions of the United Kingdom which are available at frequent intervals. In consequence unemployment has been the dominant issue in regional policy until very recently; and palliatives have been offered for unemployment blackspots instead of concentrating attention on the fostering of genuine economic growth. Likewise economists have tended to analyse unemployment when other figures might have yielded more valuable results had they been available.

The primary need is for estimates of gross domestic product to be published regularly by government for all the standard regions of the United Kingdom along with indices showing the movement of gross domestic product at constant prices. The present study shows that this is a perfectly feasible task for Scotland and previous studies have shown that it can be done for Wales and Northern Ireland.[1] The vast bulk of the work involved in all of these studies has been the building up of a method for producing the estimates. Once this is done and written up step by step, it should then be possible to bring the estimates up to date year by year with comparatively little work and much less difficulty. Ideally, this should be undertaken by government departments because they have access to a vast bulk of unpublished information which is not available to a private research worker. They also have access to Census of Production material before it is available in the normal published form. Such officially produced estimates of gross domestic product could be brought much further up to date than is possible when they are privately prepared.

For the English regions it is probable that satisfactory gross domestic product estimates could only be produced by government. Lack of data would make it extremely difficult to produce estimates of gross domestic product for these regions privately. But it seems possible that sufficient material might be available in unpublished form to enable it to be done by those who have access to it.

Without these estimates it is impossible to measure the rate of economic growth for regions, to assess the contribution of each industry to total output, to compare relative levels of output per head by regions, or to assess product per head of the working population. All of these seem basic to a proper assessment of a region's economic health. Moreover, estimates such as these would obviously be much more useful if they were available for all of Britain's standard regions, enabling comparisons to be made between them, than if they were available for only one region in isolation.

At present economic growth has to be measured by the indices of industrial production. These are only available for Scotland and Northern Ireland and they do not cover more than a part of gross domestic product. As a measure of general economic progress they are therefore unsatisfactory, while for such regions as the Midlands

[1] As this goes to be published it was learnt that official estimates of gross domestic product for Northern Ireland are being prepared.

SUMMARY OF THE MAIN FINDINGS

and the North-East no measure at all is available and little is known about their performance.

Industrial structure is normally analysed by the numbers of insured employees, since figures for working population by industries are only regularly available for Scotland and Northern Ireland. Even from the employment side this is unsatisfactory, since it excludes self-employment which plays a large part in many industries and services. Obviously a proper analysis cannot be made without a complete breakdown either of the total working population including self-employed or of the contributions of each industry and service to total output. These methods will give slightly different results since output per person employed varies from one occupation to another. Neither method is preferable to the other, the best one to choose depending on the circumstances for which an analysis of structure is required. For many regional comparisons figures of output per head by industries are required, and these can only be obtained if both working population and total output can be broken down by industries.

The section on investment in this book showed the sort of conclusions which can be reached from a study of investment and growth. To make such an analysis satisfactory, however, the statistics have to be vastly improved. The estimates of economic growth seem at present to be the weakest part. The investment figures, however, are themselves far from adequate. It is impossible at present to obtain figures for total investment by regions and the figures for manufacturing industry from the various censuses are not comparable without numerous adjustments. Clearly investment figures comparable from year to year need to be published by regions if one is to discover why some regions achieve a better economic performance than others. Figures for net investment are extremely difficult to estimate, but the analysis in Chapter 10 shows how very useful they would be. A proper regional analysis requires that one should be able to assess the productivity of investment by regions in terms both of economic growth and growth of output per head. Only then can one discover whether a region is getting enough investment, or whether the investment is being devoted to the right industries.

All the above were covered in some form in the present study. One would now like to see the estimates extended to other regions and produced regularly on an official basis. In time it should be possible to improve the quality of the estimates themselves and to extend their coverage.

In addition there are many estimates which the present study has not attempted to make, but which would be invaluable for regional economic analysis. In the first place regional figures for expenditure need to be published much more frequently and on a basis which enables them to be compared with income so that estimates of saving can be derived. Other estimates which are badly needed include the net flow of income into or out of regions, and the foreign trade multiplier as applied to regions. In the long run one may perhaps also hope to have regional input-output tables which would show the interdependence of industries in one region with those in others.

It has sometimes been asserted that saving constitutes a higher proportion of income in Scotland than in many other regions of the United Kingdom. The figures in Chapter 6 showed that income from investments formed a higher proportion of total income in Scotland than in all other regions except London and the South-East, the Southern and the South-West. This could mean simply that wealthy people came to Scotland to settle, but it could also be the result of a higher propensity to save in the past. The attempts to estimate the propensity to save in Chapter 8 were inconclusive, but there were certainly no indications that savings in Scotland formed an abnormally high proportion of income. The importance of this is that a high propensity to save, unless it is matched with equally high investment could have a depressing effect on the economy of the region. High savings would mean a lower propensity to consume than in other regions, and if the funds from these savings are not matched by investment expenditure but go to finance investment in other regions, effective demand may tend to lag behind the volume of goods and services produced.

The net flow of income into or out of Scotland was discussed in Chapter 6. It was shown that gross domestic product per head and personal income per head both expressed as a proportion of the United Kingdom were very close. Since one of these measured income arising within Scotland and the other income accruing to Scottish residents, it seemed unlikely that any net flow either into or out of Scotland was a significant proportion of the total. Even 1 per cent however could involve a flow of some £20 million or so. If Scots are receiving a larger income than that which accrues from within Scotland, then this would tend to boost effective demand; and in so far as consumer demand is satisfied by Scottish-made products, this would help the regional economy. On the other hand, if the net flow was outward, this could have a depressing effect.

Crucial to this type of analysis is the value of the foreign trade

SUMMARY OF THE MAIN FINDINGS

multiplier. An economy in which trade forms only a small proportion of total output enjoys a close relationship between the level of effective demand in the economy and the demand for goods produced in the economy. Thus if incomes rise, for whatever reason, one would expect this to stimulate production in accordance with the normal multiplier process. For a region, however, the situation is rather different. A large part of demand within the region both for consumer and investment goods is met by imports from other regions and a large proportion of the products of domestic production go to satisfy the requirements of other regions. In consequence the level of effective demand within the region does not have such a large impact on domestic production as it does in an economy with a high level of self-sufficiency.

The importance of the propensity to save or of a net flow of income into or out of the region will therefore depend on the value of the foreign trade multiplier. This will also determine the effect of a government programme of public investment. The Government are at present proposing to step up their public investment in Scotland to £140 million a year, but it is quite impossible to assess the consequences of this.[1] Much of the initial £140 million may be spent on imported materials and one cannot say how much will have an impact on the regional economy. Moreover, even if one knew that say £100 million would be spent within the region to accrue as income to its inhabitants, one does not know how much of their resulting consumption expenditure would be spent on goods produced within the region. Clearly, it would be of great value to have estimates which would show the proportion of goods imported into the region for a typical £100 of consumption expenditure. Similar estimates would be required for various types of investment expenditure, such as housing, road building, etc. Without these figures no quantitative estimates can be made of the effects of larger public expenditure or increased real incomes in Scotland or any other region.

These are but some of the more important estimates which would be required if planning at the regional level is to be properly undertaken. Planning of a sort, of course, exists today and is exemplified by the recent White Papers on Scotland and the North-East.[2] But without proper data the only planning which is possible is the general direction of government policy, the listing of priorities and the amount of expenditure which it is hoped will be made available. It is quite impossible to assess the effects of the Government's proposals.

[1] *Central Scotland: A Programme for Development and Growth*, Cmnd. 2188.
[2] Cmnd. 2188 and Cmnd. 2206.

Yet this is essential to a proper planning system: the Government should be able to assess not only the relative merits of different measures in some quantifiable way, but also forecast the amount of stimulus which a given increase in expenditure or investment is likely to create. None of these things can be done until a revolution takes place in the provision of regional statistics.

CHAPTER 12

THE IMPLICATIONS FOR POLICY

IT was not the main purpose of this book to discuss general policy issues. It would therefore be neither helpful nor appropriate to venture on to the ground already covered by the Toothill Committee and the recent White Papers.[1] There are, however, certain policy implications arising from the figures presented here, and some of the proposals announced by the Government assume a new light if seen against the background of these estimates.

The main objective of policy as seen in the White Papers is the provision of employment in Scotland and the North-East, sufficient to take account of natural increase, reduce unemployment and migration and raise participation rates. As shown by the present study an equally important objective could be the promotion of economic growth to enable Scottish gross domestic product per head of the population to approach the United Kingdom level.

It may be useful to consider what this would involve. In the first place it would imply an increase in gross domestic product per head from £377 to £431, a rise of approximately 14 per cent on 1960 figures. This is almost as much as the economic growth achieved in Scotland in the years 1951–60. But, because of lower levels of participation, the difference in gross domestic product per head of working population in employment is much smaller. On this basis the United Kingdom is only 6 per cent ahead of Scotland. To enable Scotland to catch up with the United Kingdom, therefore, the provision of employment for the unemployed and the raising of the participation rates with current levels of output per head would itself give Scotland an increase in gross domestic product per head of about 8 per cent.[2] If the United Kingdom level was to be

[1] *Report on the Scottish Economy*, Scottish Council 1961. *Central Scotland: A Programme for Development and Growth*, Cmnd. 2188, H.M.S.O., Edinburgh, Nov. 1963. *The North-East: A Programme for Regional Development and Growth*, Cmnd. 2206. H.M.S.O., London, Nov. 1963.

[2] This assumes that the ratio of working population to total population in Scotland could be made to equal the U.K. ratio. This may be unrealistic if there is a difference in age structure.

reached, therefore, productivity would only have to rise 6 per cent.

It should be emphasized, however, that these estimates are based on the 1960 situation. Meantime natural increase causes the population to grow and a certain amount of growth is required to prevent the differential between United Kingdom and Scottish product per head from widening. The growth of output of 14 per cent already referred to would therefore have to be superimposed on such growth as is required merely to maintain the *status quo*.

In the past decade, 1951–61, the actual population of Scotland only increased 1·6 per cent compared with 4·9 per cent for the United Kingdom. Thus, it would seem that Scotland's economic growth would not need to have been so rapid as that of the United Kingdom if the 1951 differential in product per head was to have been retained. The actual growth achieved by the United Kingdom between 1951 and 1960 was 26·3 per cent as measured by gross domestic product at constant prices; the growth in product per head was 20·5 per cent. Scottish economic growth totalled 17·2 per cent in the same period; and the growth in product per head was 14·8 per cent. Therefore, given the rate of emigration and the consequent slow growth of the Scottish population, Scottish gross domestic product would have had to rise only by 22 or 23 per cent compared with the United Kingdom's 26·3 per cent, if a growth in product per head of 20·5 per cent, equivalent to the United Kingdom's rate, was to have been achieved.

This calculation, of course, assumes that migration would have continued during the period 1951–60 at the same rate, even if the rate of growth had been higher. This is unlikely, and indeed it is one of the objects of policy to be able to promote growth to the point at which migration can be reduced. Scotland's net loss of population from migration during the decade averaged 25·5 thousand a year. If this migration had not taken place, Scotland's rate of economic growth would have had to be similar to the United Kingdom's even to maintain the differential in product per head. Migration has had a double effect: it has prevented the unemployment level from rising even higher; and the disparity in product per head between Scotland and the United Kingdom has not widened as much as it would otherwise have done.

If this differential is to be reduced, say over the next ten years, and if the net loss from migration is to be cut down, Scotland would clearly have to aim for a higher rate of growth than that achieved by the United Kingdom. It is impossible to estimate a precise target rate without knowing the rate which the United Kingdom will manage

THE IMPLICATIONS FOR POLICY

to achieve. But if the United Kingdom accepts 4 per cent a year as a target rate, Scotland would need to aim at between 5 and 6 per cent if a serious impact is to be made on the problem. This would be in marked contrast to the 1·9 per cent per annum achieved in the period 1951–60.

The policy most likely to achieve this, as seems now to be generally agreed, is the encouragement and inducement of the newer 'science based' industries to set up in Scotland. In the past decade it would seem that Scotland invested heavily in many of the older traditional industries, notably coal-mining and shipbuilding. Probably this was necessary to save these industries from extinction, but this type of investment does not normally achieve economic growth. Its main purpose is to cut costs to ensure the continuance of the same or a similar volume of output. It may result in higher labour productivity and lower employment. The conclusions in Chapter 10 seemed to indicate that Scottish investment had this tendency: in relation to the volume of investment the return in terms of increased productivity was good, better than for the United Kingdom. Increased productivity is clearly important, but it is not the primary need in the present state of the Scottish economy. Priority needs to be given to investment which will generate growth of output and result in higher employment. Coal and shipbuilding cannot do this, and one needs to look instead to the newer industries where an expansion in the market may be expected.

This point was clearly much in the minds of the Toothill Committee and it obviously underlies the Government thinking in the recent White Papers for Central Scotland and North-East England.[1] The main change in Government policy is that the promotion of economic growth is now the primary aim rather than provision of relief for unemployment blackspots. The level of employment depends on the pace of economic growth and it is now thought better, therefore, to go all out for the latter by providing every form of encouragement.

Government policy may be summed up as the provision of an environment which encourages growth. The development of 'growth areas' which are thought to have particularly good prospects, the rehabilitation of older industrial centres, the building of improved communications and the expanded inducements which are now offered are all part of this policy. The new approach does seem more likely to achieve the economic growth and create the employment which is required; but much depends on the way in which the Government implement their proposals and the position on the scale

[1] Op. cit.

of national economic priorities which is assigned to regional development.

The Scottish economy can only regain its economic health eventually if the structural changes envisaged are carried out. But this will take a considerable time. In the immediate present the problems of unemployment and emigration are likely to remain, largely because the need for structural readjustment was not foreseen soon enough nor pursued with sufficient vigour.

The most awkward aspect of this short-term problem is that the expansion of any industry, even if it is possible, will run into shortages of various types of labour. A situation arises in which expansion is limited by shortages of particular skills; but unemployment, especially of unskilled workers, continues at a high rate. The easy way to get round this immediate problem is to bolster up the declining industries for which the labour is adapted. But this may lead to even worse difficulties since it retards the structural adjustment in the economy which is essential to economic health in the long run. It also leads to a wasteful allocation of resources, since labour and capital are retained to produce goods the demand for which is stagnant or declining unless it is bolstered up. The production of other goods for which there is a greater need may be prevented from expanding owing to lack of resources. In very acute circumstances the bolstering of declining industries as a short-term form of relief may be justified, but only if it is not allowed to impede in any way the long-term readjustment. It may be that the Government's loans to shipping companies, which have certainly helped the shipbuilding industry, come into this category.

The industry which must in many respects play the key role in Scottish economic development is construction. This has been recognized in the Government's recent proposals for Central Scotland.[1] Not only does the creation of new towns and an improved infrastructure depend on the construction industry's ability to step up output; but the expansion of the industry which this would imply must have a direct impact on the economy. In view of this it is worth considering the position of the industry in some detail.

Construction is one of the industries over which public authorities wield a large measure of direct and indirect control. It can, therefore, be induced to expand more readily than many types of manufacturing industry which have to be attracted to Scotland, and it should be able to play an important part in meeting the short-term problem. Not even it, however, is exempt from the difficulties mentioned

[1] Cmnd. 2188.

THE IMPLICATIONS FOR POLICY

above. Expansion cannot be undertaken if the requisite skills are not available and training takes a long, perhaps an absurdly long, time.

But the situation is probably no worse than for any other industry and possibly a little better. In some branches of construction the skilled trades required are similar to those in shipbuilding; for example joiners can go from one industry to the other with comparative ease. In addition the prospect of a technical revolution in the construction industry is at last beginning to open up with the use of industrialized building methods. Such techniques are to be adopted in the new town of Livingston. This may overcome some of the existing bottlenecks and get round the time period required for training to skilled trades in the traditional construction industry.

In 1960 construction accounted for 6·4 per cent of Scottish gross domestic product with an output of £125 million. It employed 167 thousand, about 7 per cent of the total working population. Compared with some other European countries these are rather modest proportions; for example in all the Common Market countries other than France construction contributed 7 per cent or more to gross domestic product in 1960.[1] On this basis alone, therefore, it would seem reasonable to suppose that Scotland could support a larger construction industry.

The Government envisage an expansion of the industry by one-third, and it is important to consider some of the implications of this.[2] Assuming the present ratio of employment to output, this would seem to involve the additional employment of some 56 thousand. Setting this against unemployment of 90 to 100 thousand, the difference would only be some 35–40 thousand. If unemployment were reduced to this level it would amount to only 1·5 per cent of the working population. This is a level, below which it is not normally thought possible to reduce unemployment.

Obviously this comparison is not entirely valid. The economic situation is developing all the time and the potential labour force is expanding. Moreover the calculation takes no account of increased participation rates or the provision of jobs to stem migration. To meet these needs expansion in other fields is obviously required. Most important of all the figures ignore the effect of improvements in productivity which may be expected to take place in construction. Nevertheless the calculation does illustrate the scale of the operation the Government seem to be contemplating for the construction industry and the sort of impact it might have if successful. This latter

[1] O.E.C.D. General Statistics.
[2] Cmnd. 2188.

qualification is all important. It may well be found that the expansion envisaged never takes place because the labour available is not suitable. Expansion may well be held up for lack of suitable labour. Or it may take place only to the extent that it can attract labour from other industries or train young labour. Retraining seems to be the key to this problem and without it any effort to reduce the unemployment would fail. This has nothing to do with the construction industry in particular, it is a problem which would arise no matter what industry was to achieve expansion.

Growth of output by a third would raise gross domestic product by about £42 million. This in itself would be sufficient to raise 1960 gross domestic product by 2 per cent, and if there was a multiplier effect on other industries the increase would be greater than this. Construction as at present organized has an output per head which is below the average for the economy. This is particularly true of Scotland, and it is frequently argued from this that expansion of this industry would achieve less in terms of growth than some others.[1] Against this it is clear that construction is more readily expanded than manufacturing industry, because of its direct reliance on government policy, and one hopes that as a result of new methods the level of output per head will improve. If this happened a greater contribution to growth could be expected with the same increase in employment.

From these figures it seems that this policy might be more successful in absorbing unemployment than in promoting sufficient economic growth to close the gap in product per head between Scotland and the United Kingdom. Of course this would no longer be true if productivity in construction could be substantially improved. But this is not such a serious drawback in a policy for the short-term. The immediate need is to find a suitable way of absorbing unemployment; construction seems capable of making an important contribution towards this.

It may be thought that this is simply a stop-gap policy designed to meet the needs of the short-term. If it was, it might still be the right policy, since it could probably do more to improve social and living conditions in Scotland than any bolstering of demand for traditional industries. But it is much more than this. As the White Paper illustrates it occupies an essential part in the promotion of long-term growth and structural change. In the Government's view, without the building of new towns and the rehabilitation of older areas which are to become growth points, the long-term growth may not take

[1] See Chapter 2, Table V.

place and will certainly be much impeded. The role of the construction industry is to set the stage.

One may summarize this policy by saying that it relies primarily on inducement and the creation of an environment favourable to growth. Coupled with this is the direct effect of Government investment in the region; and supplementing it are various controls exercised over development in other parts of the United Kingdom. It is to be hoped that the next step will be to prepare detailed studies of Scotland's key industries with a view to assessing their prospects for expansion and thereby estimating the amount of new development that is required. Studies of this type would be essential if a proper regional plan is to be prepared.

All this may seem a rather indirect way of promoting regional development, and not even those who drew up the proposals could say with any accuracy how great their effect is likely to be. But although different Governments may make adjustments to the particular controls and inducements, it would seem that regional policy is bound to have these basic characteristics in a free economy. The fundamental problem is to raise the level of investment in the region and to ensure that that investment which does take place makes the maximum contribution to economic growth. This cannot be done by compulsion; the only course is some mixture of inducement and control.

It is therefore of the utmost importance that the effects of the measures adopted should be capable of measurement. Without this, inadequate measures may be continued too long without change, investment may be concentrated on the wrong industries or in the wrong places, or the points of weakness and growth in the economy may be unidentified. Proper analysis of the state of the regional economy is therefore essential. It cannot be claimed that this book offered a complete analysis of this type; but it must be hoped that in time it will be possible to improve and expand the provision of regional economic statistics.

A NOTE ON THE REVISION OF THE INDEX OF INDUSTRIAL PRODUCTION

An early draft of Chapter 5 was sent to the Scottish Statistical Office for comment and it was then discovered that the Office was in the process of revising the index of industrial production. Unfortunately the revised figures were not available until several months after this book went to print and it was therefore impossible to amend the text to take account of the changes. The new figures were still unpublished at the time that the proofs were being corrected, but it was clear from information received from the Scottish Statistical Office that rather drastic changes were to be made. Figures for 1960 were not finalized, but the information for 1958 shows substantial revisions. Manufacturing output as a whole is estimated to be 106 per cent of the 1954 level in 1958 and the 1960 figure, while still subject to correction, will probably be about 114 per cent. The previous estimates were 102 and 109 per cent respectively. The chief industries to be affected by the changes are as follows (1958 figures 1954=100):

	NEW INDEX	OLD INDEX
Food, Drink and Tobacco	121	108
Metal Manufacture	97	90
Engineering and Electrical	115	110
Metal Goods	107	104
Leather	84	87
Clothing	114	105
Bricks, Pottery, Glass	97	101
Timber and Furniture	84	88

That such a drastic revision in the index should be necessary hardly increases one's confidence in official statistics, especially when one considers the weight normally attached to the index in all discussions of Scotland's economic development. But the fault is not with those who, with insufficient personnel or resources, are responsible for the existing series; the real problem is that the Government have devoted a quite inadequate amount of attention to the provision of regional statistics.

The part of this book to be most affected by the changes is Chapter 5 where an attempt was made to derive estimates of the rate of price increase by industries based on the unrevised index of industrial production. In fact this exercise led to such curious results that the main conclusion was that the index must be unsatisfactory. The new calculations give much more realistic results. The rate of price change for manufacturing as a whole between 1954 and 1958 is now 17 per cent instead of 23 per cent; this compares with the United Kingdom rate of 18 per cent. The individual industry rates are likewise much more reasonable.

The majority of industries now show lower rates of price increase, the main reductions being in food, drink and tobacco, metal manufacture and clothing. In addition, information received from the Scottish Statistical Office indicates that the high rate of price increase previously calculated for shipbuilding and marine engineering was due to an error in the figure for Scotland in the 1958 Census of Production. The new estimates of price increase by industries are as follows with the old estimates shown in brackets:

Price Increases 1954–58 (1954=100)

Food, Drink and Tobacco	118 (131·7)
Chemicals, etc.	106 (107·6)
Metal Manufacture	137 (147·5)
Engineering and Electrical	117 (122·1)
Shipbuilding, etc.	121 (121·1)
Vehicles	119 (149·3)
Metal goods	123 (126·5)
Textiles	108 (109·4)
Leather	112 (107·4)
Clothing	114 (122·4)
Bricks, etc.	123 (117·8)
Timber, etc.	112 (106·8)
Paper, etc.	114 (116·7)
Other manufacturing	111 (114·8)
Total manufacturing	117 (123·1)

The analysis in Chapter 10, which tried to relate the growth of output to investment, likewise relied heavily on the index of industrial production. The main effect of the changes here is to show the Scottish economy in a rather more favourable light. The old index had shown Scotland with a very poor rate of growth in relation to a gross investment ratio of 9·6 from 1951–58. The new index gives Scotland a rate of growth of 2·0 per cent a year instead of 1·3 per cent; this gives a gross marginal capital/output ratio of 4·8 instead of 7·4 (see page 109). This puts Scotland on a par with the United Kingdom, though not in quite such a favourable position as Wales or Northern Ireland. The comparisons based on net investment are less affected, since the revision of the rate of growth also alters the calculation of the net investment ratio. The new figures are 3·4 for the net investment ratio instead of 2·4, but the marginal capital/output ratio changes only from 1·8 to 1·7 (see page 112). The comparison of net investment and productivity is even less affected, the investment/productivity ratio remaining at 1·4. The conclusions of the chapter are therefore unaffected.

APPENDIX

SOURCES AND METHODS

The abbreviations listed below are used in the Appendix on the following pages:

D.S.S.   Digest of Scottish Statistics, H.M.S.O., Edinburgh.
A.A.S.   Annual Abstract of Statistics, H.M.S.O., London.
B.B.   National Income & Expenditure (Blue Book), H.M.S.O., London.
Sources & Methods   National Income Statistics: Sources & Methods, H.M.S.O., London, 1956.

APPENDIX

PART I: GROSS DOMESTIC PRODUCT AND THE OUTPUT OF
MANUFACTURING INDUSTRY

THE estimates for the Gross Domestic Product of Scotland were obtained by adding the contribution of each major industry or occupation. These were divided in the same way as shown in the Blue Book table *Gross Domestic Product by Industry and Type of Income*.[1]

This is not the normal practice in making estimates of the Gross Domestic Product of an economy. The usual procedure is to aggregate the totals for employment income, gross trading profits, gross trading surpluses of public corporations and rent. For most economies this can be done from inland revenue data and from the accounts of public corporations. The division of Gross Domestic Product between groups of industries and occupations then becomes a secondary exercise; and the direct estimate of Gross Domestic Product may even differ very slightly from the sum of the estimates by industry and type of income.

This is broadly speaking the way in which United Kingdom estimates are built up. It approximates also to the procedure used by Campbell for his estimates of the National Income of Scotland and by Cuthbert in making similar estimates for Northern Ireland.[2] Clearly, this method could have been used for Scotland; but it seemed that it would be less accurate than the addition of estimates for each industry and sector. This latter method approximates to that used by Carter and Robson for Northern Ireland and by Nevin for Wales.[3]

There are various reasons for preferring this method. In the first place inland revenue figures are not available in the same detail for Scotland as they are for the United Kingdom, at any rate in published form. Furthermore, the inland revenue figures which are available are much less satisfactory as a basis for compiling regional estimates than for national estimates. Any difference between the place of assessment and the region to which the income may properly be said to accrue is unimportant in compiling national estimates; but it may play havoc with regional estimates. The main difficulty here arises over Schedule D. National figures for gross trading profits of companies are compiled with heavy reliance on the inland revenue assessments of income under Schedule D. Schedule D figures are of course published for Scotland; and in this Scotland has an

[1] *National Income and Expenditure, 1962* (Table 16).

[2] A. D. Campbell, 'Changes in Scottish Incomes, 1924–49', *Economic Journal*, Vol. LXV, 1955, p. 225; N. Cuthbert, 'Total Civilian Income in Northern Ireland', Appendix A in *An Economic Survey of Northern Ireland* by K. S. Isles and N. Cuthbert, H.M.S.O., Belfast, 1957, also in Journal of the Statistical and Social Inquiry Society of Ireland, 104th Session, 1951.

[3] Professor C. F. Carter and Mary Robson, *A Comparison of the National Incomes Social Accounts of Northern Ireland, the Republic of Ireland and the United Kingdom*, Journal of the Statistical and Social Inquiry Society of Ireland, Vol. XIX, 1954–55, pp. 62–87. Edward Nevin (editor), *The Social Accounts of the Welsh Economy, 1948–56*, University of Wales Press, 1957.

advantage over most of the other regions of the United Kingdom. But the firms assessed under Schedule D in Scotland are not necessarily all the firms contributing to the Gross Domestic Product of Scotland. For instance, branches of English firms operating in Scotland may for tax purposes be assessed at the head office in England; yet they make a contribution to the Scottish Gross Domestic Product.[1]

So that this problem may be minimized, estimates have been based as far as possible on the *Census of Production* and on such other sources as give figures for income under the region in which it originates.[2] This meant that Schedule D figures did not have to be used for the estimates of manufacturing industry, the sector where the greatest error seemed likely to arise.

It will be noticed that the definitions used in the United Kingdom *National Income and Expenditure* vary considerably over the decade, the largest change taking place in 1959 when the revised Standard Industrial Classification was adopted.[3] As far as possible the estimates presented in this book have been made comparable with the definitions used in *National Income and Expenditure 1958*. As a result it has sometimes been necessary to make adjustments to United Kingdom figures for later years.

I. AGRICULTURE, FORESTRY AND FISHING

The contribution of agriculture to the Gross Domestic Product can be estimated accurately and without much difficulty from figures published annually in *Scottish Agricultural Economics*.[4] This publication gives the gross output of Scottish agriculture together with the principal items of expenditure and details of production grants and subsidies. All forms of price support are included in the figures for gross output.

The contribution to Gross Domestic Product consists of the net income of farmers, payments to employees, rent, interest and depreciation.[5] Net income of farmers as normally defined is not given in *Scottish Agricultural Economics*, but can be obtained by subtracting the main items of expenditure from gross output plus production grants and subsidies. This should give a figure comparable to that published for the U.K. in the *Annual Review and Determination of Guarantees*.[6] To this is then added payments

[1] This problem is much less serious for estimates of income accruing to residents such as those made by Professor Campbell and Mr Cuthbert (op. cit.). For such studies it is not necessary to estimate gross trading profits of companies, but only income accruing from interest and dividends to individuals. This was not possible in making estimates of Gross Domestic Product.

[2] The *Reports on the Census of Production 1951 to 1958*, Board of Trade, London. H.M.S.O.

[3] *National Income and Expenditure*, Yearly. Central Statistical Office, London. H.M.S.O.

[4] H.M.S.O., Edinburgh.

[5] *Sources and Methods*, p. 94.

[6] See, for instance, *Annual Review and Determination of Guarantees, 1962*. Cmnd. 1658, pp. 14 and 15.

APPENDIX

to labour, rent, interest and depreciation. The total represents the contribution of agriculture to Gross Domestic Product, and it remains only to adjust the estimates to a calendar year basis.

The contribution of forestry and fishing was very much more difficult to estimate than that of agriculture. The *Annual Report of the Forestry Commissioners* gives no separate information on Scotland which can be used as a basis for estimates, and figures for the fishing industry are equally difficult to obtain. In *B.B.* agriculture, forestry and fishing are all presented together, so that even for the United Kingdom separate estimates of the contributions of forestry and fishing are not available. Even the data for total manpower engaged in these industries in the United Kingdom is not given separately for each industry.

Such data as were available from published sources showed insured employees in each of the three industries separately (*A.A.S.* and *D.S.S.*); the value of fish landed in Scotland and in England and Wales (*A.A.S.*); the income assessed under Schedule D for forestry and fishing together, both for the United Kingdom and for Scotland (Inland Revenue Reports); and the employment income of forestry and fishing in the United Kingdom assessed under Schedule E (Inland Revenue Reports). In addition the Statistics Office of the Inland Revenue kindly supplied assessments of income from employment under Schedule E for forestry and fishing in Scotland over the period 1950–51 to 1960–61.

It was clear that with such information as was available from published sources only a very crude estimate could be attempted. Yet forestry and fishing are of considerable importance to the Scottish economy and play a much larger part there than they do in England and Wales. The figures for insured employees showed that during the 1950s Scotland had between 36 and 38 per cent of United Kingdom employees in fishing and just over 30 per cent of those in forestry.

Fortunately with the aid of the Scottish Schedule E figures supplied by the Inland Revenue a reasonably satisfactory estimate could be made.

The procedure adopted was first to find the contribution of forestry and fishing to the Gross Domestic Product of the United Kingdom. This was done by estimating agriculture and subtracting this from the total shown under agriculture, forestry and fishing.[1] Estimates for agriculture can be made in the same way as those already described for Scotland from information available both in *A.A.S.* and in the *Annual Review and Determination of Guarantees*. The results of these calculations are shown in Table I. The subtraction of the estimate for agriculture from the figures given in *B.B.* gave a residual which represented the contribution of forestry and fishing in the United Kingdom, this varied between £46 million and £64 million during the decade.

Estimates for Scotland could now be derived by applying a ratio to the United Kingdom figures. Scottish income assessed under Schedules D and

---

[1] See, for instance, *National Income and Expenditure, 1962* (Table 16).

TABLE I
Agriculture, Forestry and Fishing
Contribution to G.D.P. £ million

	1951	1952	1953	1954	1955	1956	1957	1958	1959	1960
United Kingdom										
Agriculture, Forestry & Fishing (BB)	726	770	786	776	800	822	863	873	880	919
Agriculture	673	720	740	719	752	769	812	809	829	867
Forestry & Fishing (by subtraction)	53	50	46	57	48	53	51	64	51	52
Scotland										
Agriculture	83	94	93	89	86	95	98	97	96	99
Forestry & Fishing	14	13	12	14	13	15	14	15	13	14
TOTAL	97	107	105	103	99	110	112	112	109	113

Scotland
Inland Revenue Data (Forestry and Fishing)
£ million

	1950-51	'51-52	'52-53	'53-54	'54-55	'55-56	'56-57	'57-58	'58-59	'59-60	'60-61
Schedule E	2.7	2.9	2.9	3.1	3.3	3.7	3.6	3.8	3.7	3.8	4.3
Schedule D	4.1	5.1	4.0	3.9	3.5	5.2	6.1	5.7	4.7	5.3	—
TOTAL	6.8	8.0	6.9	7.0	6.8	8.9	9.7	9.5	8.4	9.1	—
as % of U.K.	29.4	25.6	26.7	26.1	24.5	27.2	28.8	27.4	24.1	25.3	26

APPENDIX

E was expressed as a proportion of the equivalent income for the United Kingdom. This ratio was then applied to the United Kingdom income of forestry and fishing derived as a residual from *B.B.* This gave an estimate for Scotland which varied between 25 and 29 per cent of United Kingdom income (see Table I). The Scottish ratio of income under Schedule E was lower than the Schedule D ratio: the former varying between 15 and 17 per cent while the latter was always greater than a third and sometimes as high as a half. This seems to reflect the character of the Scottish fishing industry where a lower proportion of the total manpower relied on fixed wages and salaries than is customary in the rest of the United Kingdom.

It is interesting to compare the ratio derived from the data with some of the ratios obtainable from published sources. A ratio derived from the value of fish landed, for instance, varies between 24 and 29 per cent, very close to the income ratio from the data. The ratio of insured employees on the other hand is much higher. This makes the Schedule E ratio of 15–17 per cent somewhat surprising. It seems clear that the income of employees in Scotland in the form of wages and salaries is substantially below the United Kingdom level; but it is probable that many of those classified as employees also receive a share in profits from income assessed under Schedule D.

II. MANUFACTURING, MINING AND QUARRYING, GAS, ELECTRICITY AND WATER

The basic source of these industries was the *Censuses of Production*. At the time of writing, these covered the years 1951–58, but only three of these were detailed, 1951, 1954 and 1958. For the intermediate years only sample censuses were available. For 1959 and 1960 no censuses were available and the method adopted was to relate the Scottish Index of Industrial Production (*D.S.S.*) to 1958 figures and adjust as far as possible by the appropriate price changes.

In most years it would have been possible to work in terms of a total of all manufacturing industries without giving any breakdown for industrial order groups. Indeed this would have been much simpler, since the division between order groups caused a large amount of additional work. The exceptions to this are the years 1952 and 1953 and 1959 and 1960, where totals could only be obtained by adding the estimates made for each order. It may be that in future estimates could be made in this way, thereby short-cutting much of the work. But for this study it was felt that totals for each order were of considerable interest and it was decided to subject them to analysis in Chapter 4. Estimates were therefore built up for each order group in manufacturing industry for all the years covered by the study.

(a) *1951, 1954 and 1958*
The best estimates are clearly those for 1951, 1954 and 1958; but even these required substantial adjustments. Each detailed census is slightly

different in coverage and in scope from the previous one and each one had to be adjusted before comparison could be made with the others. It was decided to adopt the definitions of the 1954 Census as far as possible and to adjust the others to this basis. The biggest adjustment arose in converting the 1958 Census to the 1948 Standard Industrial Classification, which was used for all the earlier censuses. Fortunately the 1958 Census gave comparative figures for 1954 under the new Standard Industrial Classification. By comparing these with the figures given for net output in the 1954 Census it was possible to construct a bridge for converting the 1958 Census figures to the 1954 basis (see Table II).

Apart from the change in the Standard Industrial Classification, there were also some differences in coverage between 1954 and 1958. Details of this are given in *Guides to Official Sources, No. 6: Census of Production Reports*.[1] The bridge constructed to adjust the 1958 figure to 1954 basis automatically made a rough adjustment for this; but in the case of repair establishments working mainly for the trade which had been included in previous reports a separate estimate was made. In general, the method adopted for converting 1958 figures to the 1954 basis seemed some way short of satisfactory; and as a result it is likely that the 1958 figures are rather less accurate than those for 1954 and 1951. But without more published information on the changes made it seemed impossible to improve on this method; and such inaccuracies as do arise are more likely to effect individual industries than the total for manufacturing.

The 1951 Census was much more closely comparable with the 1954 Census than was 1958. The chief difference was that it only gave figures for larger establishments whereas 1954 gave figures for all establishments; this was based on the actual returns for larger establishments, plus an estimate for small firms. The procedure adopted here was to calculate the relationship between net output of larger establishments and net output of all establishments in 1954. The 1951 figures for larger establishments were then grossed up by this difference (see Table II).[2] Certain minor differences in coverage between the 1951 and 1954 Censuses also arose. The 1951 Census included tea blending and coffee roasting; laundries, dry cleaning, job dyeing and carpet beating; also wholesale slaughtering. These industries were all excluded in the 1954 Census.[3] Adjustments are automatically made for this if 1951 figures are taken from the summary tables of the 1954 Census.

[1] H.M.S.O., London, 1961.
[2] Unlike the 1954 Census the summary volumes of 1951 do not give regional figures of net output. These can be obtained for 1951 from the summary volumes of the 1954 Census or from *Analysis of Standard Regions by Trades, 1948 and 1951*, and *Analysis of Orders by Region, 1951*, available from the Statistics Division, Board of Trade.
[3] *Guides to Official Sources: No. 6—Census of Production Reports.*, H.M.S.O., London, 1961, p. 23.

APPENDIX

TABLE II

Net Output of all Firms as a percentage of net output of Larger Establishments (1954)

Conversion of 1958 Census to 1954 basis

1948 S.I.C.	RATIO	RATIO†
Order III	104·0	99·4
Order IV	103·2	97·4
Order V	120·5*	96·7
Order VI	101·4	106·3
Order VII	101·7*	123·9
Order VIII	114·6*	106·8
Order IX	109·0*	—
Order X	101·3	99·2
Order XI	114·3	100·0
Order XII	110·0*	112·7
Order XIII	110·2	114·5
Order XIV	122·1	98·2
Order XV	103·2	99·2
Order XVI	101·9*	97·7
All Manufacturing	104·2	106·3
Order II	100·9*	
Order XVIII	104·5	

Note: * Calculation excludes undisclosed trades. In Orders V, VIII, IX, only the figures for larger establishments are affected by the non-diclosure provisions. In Orders XII and XVI only the figure for all firms is affected.

In the 1958 Census Order III of the 1948 S.I.C. corresponds to Order XIII and Order XIII to III. Order VI becomes Engineering and Electrical plus Precision Instruments which were previously Order IX. Order VII is Shipbuilding, VIII Vehicles and IX Metal Goods not elsewhere specified. In the table above the figures are classified according to the 1948 S.I.C. except that Orders VI and IX of the 1948 S.I.C. are taken together.

† 1954 figures from 1954 Census ÷ 1954 figures from 1958 Census.

Source: Census of Production 1954.
Census of Production 1958.

Undisclosed Trades

For these three years, despite the detailed nature of the Censuses, difficulties arose over undisclosed trades and over trades in manufacturing industry not covered by the census. Because of the non-disclosure provisions the figures for certain trades were not published on the grounds that they might reveal information about particular firms. The figures are, however, included in the totals for manufacturing industry. In general the smaller the region the more undisclosed trades there are likely to be.

For the most part the Scottish figures are affected much less than those for Wales by these provisions, but Order VII(Vehicles) is seriously affected and there are omissions also in Orders XII(Clothing), XVI(Other Manufacturing) and II(Mining and Quarrying). For 1951 where the figures were only for larger establishments the non-disclosure provisions exacted a more serious toll. In addition to the Orders already mentioned there were omissions from V(Metal Manufacture), VIII(Metal goods not elsewhere specified) and IX(Precision Instruments). The procedure adopted for these last three Orders, which were excluded from 1951 only was to derive a grossing up factor by comparison with 1954. Using 1954 figures the total for each Order was expressed as a percentage of the 1954 total for those trades which were listed in the 1951 Census. The 1951 figures were then adjusted by this percentage. For Order V the 1951 figures had to be increased by 19·7 per cent, but for the other two orders the difference was very small: 2 per cent for Order VIII and 2·8 per cent for Order IX.

This method could not be used for the four Orders excluded from both 1951 and 1954 Censuses. But since the totals for the undisclosed trades in three of the Orders are included in the total for all manufacturing industry, the problem was one of allocation. This was not the case for Order II (Mining and Quarrying), where the slate quarries and mines were undisclosed, but the amount involved was obviously small.

The allocation between undisclosed trades in manufacturing industry was done chiefly on the basis of employment statistics. These were obtained from $D.S.S.$ figures of insured employees. The figures for unemployment should be subtracted from these figures, but this could only be done in the most approximate fashion since unemployment figures for Scotland are not published by minimum list headings. The procedure was to multiply the employment figure by the output per head of the particular undisclosed trade as given in the Census for the United Kingdom.

A problem arose over Glovemaking which was the undisclosed trade in Order XII. No separate figures for employment in glovemaking are available from $D.S.S.$ However, the 1954 Census, although it gave no total for glovemaking in the summary tables for all firms, nevertheless gave a figure for 'Hats, Caps, Millinery and Gloves' under larger establishments. The same table gave a figure for employment in small firms for these three trades together. All that was required therefore was to make an estimate of the net output of small glovemaking establishments on the basis of the employment figure which could easily be separated from the other trades. The position with cinematograph film production (Order XVI) was somewhat similar: here only small firms were involved and no estimate was available for employment. The procedure used was to subtract the total employment for those trades given in the Census from the total insured employees less unemployed given in $D.S.S.$ The residual should represent the missing trade. But owing to differences in definition between the Census and $D.S.S.$ it is possible there may be some error here. The United Kingdom figure for output per head was £1,424 in 1954. Net output was estimated at £1·4 million.

APPENDIX

Once these totals had been reached, a small adjustment was made so that the total for all the Orders together should equal the total given for all manufacturing industry. The extent of this adjustment was extremely small: in fact by multiplying employment by U.K. output per head to obtain estimates for the undisclosed trades the total was short by £0·6 million. The largest of the undisclosed trades was Locomotive Shops and Manufacturing in Order VII. The estimate made for this was £5·7 million. The figures involved for the others were very small (see Table III).

For slate mines and quarries the procedure was exactly the same except that there was no check on the total. But the amount involved was again small. Employment was taken as 1·6 thousand in 1954 and output per head as £487. This gave a net output of £0·8 million.

TABLE III
Undisclosed Trades 1954

ORDER	TRADE	NET OUTPUT	EMPLOYMENT
		£m	'000s
VII	Locomotive Shops & Manufacturing	5·7	11·8
XII	Hats, Caps, Millinery & Gloves*	0·5	0·9
XVI	Cinematograph film production	1·4	1·0†
II	Slate Quarries and Mines	0·8	1·6†
	Repair Trades		
VII	Motor Vehicle Repairing‡	13·2	20·4
XII	Boot and Shoe Repairs‡	1·4	2·6
IX	Watch and Clock Repairs	1·0	1·5

* Only Glovemaking was undisclosed (see text).
† Obtained as a residual (see text).
‡ Excluding the section of the trade included in the Census.

Repair Trades
The other principal adjustment concerned the repair trades, most of which were not covered by the Census. Once again this involved Orders VII and XII for motor vehicle repairs and boot and shoe repairs respectively. There was also the addition of watch and clock repairs to Order IX.

Order VII as given in the 1954 Census includes some of the motor vehicle repair trades but not all. This is because some of them are listed as working 'for the trade'. The procedure used for calculating the net output of the remainder was to take the employment figure from *D.S.S.*, subtract from this that section of the trade included in the Census, and multiply the employment of the remainder by the net output per head of the part given in the Census. This gave a net output of £13·2 million in 1954 in addition to the £5·4 million given in the Census.

The estimate for boot and shoe repairs was made in a similar way. Output per head was taken as £521 which gave total net output of £1·4 million.

Watch and clock repairs were more difficult because a figure for net output per head could not be obtained from any information in the Census except for watch and clock manufacturing. This figure may be very wide of the mark, but in the absence of other information it was decided to use it. Employment for watch and clock repairs was not given separately in *D.S.S.*; but an estimate was made by subtracting the Census total for other trades in Order IX from the *D.S.S.* total. This gave employment of 1·5 thousand and a net output of £1·0 million resulted. In view of the small size of the final estimate the very approximate way in which it was reached seemed unlikely to lead to any important error.

For 1951 estimates for the repair trades were made in the same way. The total for motor vehicle repairs not covered by the Census came to £9·2 million; for boot and shoe repairs £1·0 million; and for watch and clock repairs £0·7 million.

Undisclosed Trades and Repair Trades 1958

Partly because of the change in Standard Industrial Classification, and partly because trades previously undisclosed were now grouped with other trades, the 1958 Census gave no incomplete orders for Scotland. Considerable difficulty arose, however, over Order VII(vehicles). In the 1954 Census this Order had been incomplete, the missing trade being 'Railway Locomotive Shops and Locomotive Manufacturing'. In 1958 this trade was grouped with Aircraft Manufacturing, Perambulators and Handcarts, but the 1954 total for the Order in the 1958 Census differed substantially from estimates for 1954.

So far as could be seen the change in definition under the new Standard Industrial Classification left the Order substantially as it was except that all forms of motor vehicle repairing were now excluded. But the 1954 figures for net output, excluding all motor vehicle repairs and including an estimate for Locomotive Shops, etc. totalled £30·5 million. The figure given in the 1958 Census for 1954 was only £24·6 million. Unfortunately, the 1958 Census does not give the 1954 figures by trade, so that it is difficult to see where the discrepancy arose.

The simplest way to find the discrepancy would have been to check the employment figures against the figures in *D.S.S.* But unfortunately it is not possible to do this satisfactorily since the *D.S.S.* did not adopt the 1958 Standard Industrial Classification until 1959. It appears, however, that at least part of the discrepancy arises in the trade Railway Carriages, Wagons and Trams. Here employment according to the 1954 Census was 11·1 thousand, but in 1958 it was only 7·1 thousand. On the other hand according to *D.S.S.* under the 1948 Standard Industrial Classification employment in this trade rose throughout the period from 9·8 thousand to 10·2 thousand. It appears that this may be accounted for by the exclusion of a part of this trade in 1958 which was primarily engaged in repair work and therefore classified under Transport and Communication according to the new definition.[1]

The solution adopted for this problem was the same as that used for

[1] It is now understood that this discrepancy is due to an error in the Census of Production for 1958.

APPENDIX

converting other Orders in the 1958 Census to the 1954 basis. The 1954 figures, including an estimate for Locomotive Shops, etc. were 23·9 per cent above the 1954 figures given in the 1958 Census. This was taken as a measure of the difference in the definition and the 1958 figures were grossed up by this amount (see Table II).

The estimation of net output for the repair trades was much more difficult in 1958 than in 1954 or 1951. In the two previous years it was usually possible to make an estimate for that part of these trades which was excluded from the Census by referring to the part which worked 'for the trade' and was therefore included. In 1958 all the repair trades were excluded and this method was therefore no longer applicable.

The procedure adopted was to calculate the increase in net output per person employed for the rest of each order to which the repair trades belonged between 1954 and 1958. This increase was found to be 25·7 per cent for Order VII, 27·8 per cent for Order XII, and 26·0 per cent for Order IX, though this latter could only be estimated approximately owing to the change in definition. The net output of the repair trades was then adjusted by the change in employment and grossed up by the increase in net output per head applicable to the rest of each Order. This is rather an unsatisfactory procedure, since the net output of the repair trades might well rise at a different rate from the rest of the Order. Any error is likely to be very small in Orders XII and IX, but could be more serious for Order VII. The final estimates for net output of the repair trades comes to: £25·6 million for motor vehicles and cycle repairing; £1·7 million for boot and shoe repairs; and £1·3 million for watch and clock repairs.

(b) *The Intermediate Years, 1952, 1953, 1955, 1956 and 1957*

Estimates for the intermediate years are necessarily much less accurate than for those years for which a detailed census is available. During these years the census was completed on a sample basis and for Scotland only certain trades are published. There are therefore no Scottish totals by industrial orders as there are for the years in which a detailed census was taken. There is the additional complication that the coverage for 1952 and 1953 is not quite the same as for 1955, 1956 and 1957. Certain trades in Orders V, VI and XIII which are included for the two former years are not available for the latter. Furthermore the estimates for the two earlier years refer to larger establishments only whereas the others cover all establishments.

The proportion of each Order accounted for by the published trades can be calculated from the detailed censuses and the results of this based on 1954 are shown in Table IV. It will be seen that for some Orders the published trades make up a substantial proportion of the total, for others the proportion is small, and for a few none of the trades in the order are published.

The procedure adopted was to gross up the published trades for each order by the difference between their total and the total for the whole

Order as shown in the three detailed censuses. The years 1952 and 1953 were further adjusted for the inclusion of small firms on the assumption that small firms in these years contributed the same proportion to the total output of each order as they did in 1954. In most cases the proportion of the whole order made up by the published trades did not vary much between the three years 1951, 1954 and 1958. The main exceptions to this were Order VII(Vehicles), where the published trades made up a much smaller proportion of the total in 1951 than in the other two years, and Order XVI(Other Manufacturing Industry) where the proportion was lower for 1954 than for 1951 or 1958.

TABLE IV

The proportion of Industrial Orders accounted for by the Published Trades*

	1952 & '53 %	1955, '56 &'57 %
Order III	75	75
Order IV	nil	nil
Order V	84	72
Order VI	79	75
Order VII	50	50
Order VIII	43	43
Order IX	nil	nil
Order X	69	69
Order XI	nil	49
Order XII	66	66
Order XIII	61	42
Order XIV	76	76
Order XV	88	88
Order XVI	48	48
Total Manufacturing	—	96
Order II	88	88
Order XVIII	86	86

* Based on proportions from the 1954 Census.

The simplest way of estimating totals for the intermediate years would have been to apply the 1954 proportions throughout. But it was thought that this would not allow sufficiently for any change which took place in the actual proportions. Accordingly, it was decided to estimate 1952 as far as possible on 1951 proportions; 1953, 1955 and 1956 on 1954 proportions; and 1957 on 1958 proportions.

In certain cases it was not possible to follow this rule: for instance, the change in industrial classification for 1958 made it difficult to get proportions for that year which were comparable with previous years. For some Orders, therefore, 1954 proportions had to be used in estimating 1957. This applied to Orders III, XII and XIII. In other cases there was a sudden

APPENDIX

jump in the estimate for the published trades which possibly coincided with the opening of a new plant or factory. In such instances it seemed best to use the proportions based on whatever year seemed most applicable. For this reason Orders VII and XV in 1953 were estimated on the 1951 proportion and Order V for 1952 on the 1954 proportion. It was thought that the figures resulting from these calculations and adjustments could be regarded as reasonably accurate. But had the gaps between the detailed censuses been longer, this method might have led to substantial error.

For Orders IV(Chemicals), IX(Precision Instruments) and XI(Leather) the above method proved impossible since the censuses contained no published trades for Scotland. These Orders therefore had to be estimated in an entirely different way. 1954 was taken as the base year and the census estimates for this year were adjusted first by the Scottish volume index of industrial production ($D.S.S.$) and then by a price index. The application of the index of industrial production gave estimates for the other years in terms of 1954 prices and the price index was required to correct these to current prices.

The main source of error in this calculation is likely to arise in the application of the price index. There is no price index for Scottish manufacturing output let alone one for each industrial order. Even for the United Kingdom the various index numbers of wholesale prices do not correspond closely to industrial orders and are therefore difficult to apply. Of the three Orders concerned only in chemicals was the value of output likely to amount to a substantial figure. Here, fortunately, there was a price index for the United Kingdom ($A.A.S.$), and this was applied together with the Scottish volume index. Of course, if the United Kingdom price index is not representative of the output of the Scottish chemical industry, some error could result; but as a check the estimates were carried back to 1951 and forward to 1958 to see how they compared with the census figures for those years. It was found that the estimate for 1951 by this method was rather high compared with the census figure, £31 million instead of £25 million, but that the 1958 estimate compared very well with the census, £48 million as opposed to £49·5 million.

For the other two Orders it was difficult to get a representative price index even for the United Kingdom. But the value of net output was in any case so small that errors would most probably appear only in the decimal. With firm estimates for 1951, 1954 and 1958 it was therefore possible to interpolate figures for the intervening years by applying the volume index to the 1954 figure and adjusting for prices partly by guesswork and partly on the basis of such price information as was published for appropriate trades ($A.A.S.$).

The total for manufacturing industry was obtained by adding the estimates for individual orders. But for 1955, 1956, and 1957 a total was also available for manufacturing industry from the census. On the basis of 1954, for which figures were also published in the sample censuses, this total was 96 per cent of the figure obtained in the detailed census. For these three years, therefore, this figure acts as a check on the totals reached by addition. Owing to the various adjustments and additions made for repair trades, etc. the census total even in the 1954 Census is somewhat lower than the final estimates used in this study. The 1954 figure in the sample censuses is lower still and amounts to 93·6 per cent of these final estimates. For the other three years, 1955, 1956 and 1957, the total figure for manufacturing industry given in the sample census amounts to 96·2 per cent, 93·2 per cent and 93·4 per cent of the estimates made here for each of the years respectively.

The estimates for 1956 and 1957 therefore seem to be very similar, whether the total is reached by adding the estimates for each Order, or simply by grossing up the census figure for manufacturing industry on the basis of the 1954 estimate. Only for 1955 was there any significant discrepancy between the two methods. Here it seemed possible that the estimate obtained by addition of the Order totals was too low, since the total figure published in the census came to 96·2 per cent of the estimate which was more than 2 per cent above the corresponding 1954 figures.

The total figure for manufacturing in the sample census seemed more likely to be accurate than the estimated total reached by addition. It was therefore decided to revise the latter so that the census total came to the same percentage of the final estimate as it did in 1954. The estimate was therefore raised so that the census total came to 93·6 per cent of the final estimate. The adjustment was distributed between orders on a percentage basis. Since 1955 was the only year, of that those could be checked, in which such a discrepancy arose, it seemed likely that the estimates for 1952 and 1953, which could not be checked in this way, could be regarded as reasonably accurate.

(c) *1959 and 1960*

At the time this study was in progress, no census material had been published for 1959 and 1960. Estimates for these years are therefore rather less satisfactory than for the others. The only way in which figures could be obtained at all was by using the 1958 estimates as a base and applying to them first the Scottish index of industrial production and secondly a price index. This was the same method as that applied in the intermediate years to those orders which were not covered by the sample censuses. The difficulties encountered were the same: the principle one being the absence of a price index for Scotland and the difficulty of even getting adequate price data for the United Kingdom.

The total for manufacturing industry could be estimated in two ways. First, it could be estimated directly by grossing up the 1958 total first by the volume index of industrial production for Scotland (*D.S.S.*) to get output at 1958 prices, and then by the wholesale price index for United Kingdom manufacturing industry (*A.A.S.*). Alternatively, one could proceed in a similar way with each industrial order and derive manufacturing industry from the addition of the Order totals.

APPENDIX

Estimates were in fact obtained by both methods, but it appeared that the second was preferable. The difficulty arises from the application of United Kingdom price indices. Simply to take the United Kingdom price index for manufacturing industry as a whole does not allow for the rather different composition of manufacturing output in Scotland. And it may well be that because of this the prices of Scottish manufacturing output as a whole change at a different rate from United Kingdom prices. To improve on this the calculation was done by industrial Orders. This takes account of the different weighting of Scottish output by orders; but error may still arise in so far as the weighting of Scottish output by trades within orders is different from the United Kingdom.

In fact when the two methods were tried the difference in the estimates for manufacturing output turned out to be very small. It appeared, therefore, that such difference as Scotland had in the composition of her output *by orders* was not such as to make Scottish prices behave very differently from those of the United Kingdom.

At the trade level, however, the different composition of output may be more serious. There is some evidence that this is so. As a check on the accuracy of the methods used for 1959 and 1960, they were applied to earlier years to see how the results compared with the census estimates. Using 1954 as a base, estimates for manufacturing output in 1958 were derived first by applying the Scottish index of industrial production (manufacturing industries) and the price index for the United Kingdom. The figure which resulted was £640 millions as opposed to £720 millions based on the census, a difference of 11 per cent. If this difference cannot be put down to the composition of Scottish output by orders, then presumably it is due to Scotland's different composition by trades as compared with the United Kingdom, unless one is prepared to accept that the official index of industrial production is inaccurate.[1]

From this it followed that the method used for 1959 and 1960 may give a figure which is somewhat too low. The error is not likely to be so great as in the calculation of 1958 on a 1954 base, because in this case the estimate covers only two years instead of four. Moreover it was a period when prices were comparatively stable: whereas the United Kingdom price index for manufactured goods rose 11 per cent between 1954 and 1958, it rose only 1·8 per cent between 1958 and 1960.[2] It seems probable, therefore, that in the estimates for 1959 and 1960 a much larger proportion of the increase in output will be accounted for by an increase in volume than was the case for the period 1954–58. If this is so, any error which arises from the application of United Kingdom price indices to Scotland will be much less than in the earlier period.

The main difficulty in making estimates for each Order was to get price series applicable by Orders even for the United Kingdom. In fact only for a few Orders, II, X, XI, XII, and XIV was it possible to use the United King-

[1] See Chapter 5 where this question is dealt with in detail.
[2] *Annual Abstract of Statistics, 1962.*

dom index of wholesale prices (*A.A.S.*). For the other orders an index had to be constructed. This was done in a rather approximate fashion. The contribution of each Order to G.D.P. for 1958, 1959 and 1960 in the United Kingdom was estimated by adding wages, salaries and gross trading profits as shown in *B.B.* The figures were deflated by the volume index of industrial production for the United Kingdom (*A.A.S.*), and the remaining figures were taken to show the change in prices over the period of the 1958 volume of output. The price indices resulting from these calculations are shown in Table V.

TABLE V

Price Indices Used in the Estimation of Net Output 1959 and 1960

1958=100

1948 s.i.c.	1959	1960
Order III	103·0	109·9
Order IV	101·1	94·1
Order V	106·0	102·6
Order VI†	100·0	100·7
‡	103·0	112·8
Order VII	100·1	102·2
Order VIII	102·6	104·4
Order IX	—	—
Order X*	97·5	102·5
Order XI*	122·9	117·6
Order XII*	99·7	101·5
Order XIII	101·3	102·5
Order XIV*	98·4	101·4
Order XV	100·1	99·3
Order XVI	100·6	100·8
Order II*	98·4	99·8
Order XVIII	105·9	104·6

† Engineering, Electrical and Precision Instruments.
‡ Shipbuilding and Marine Engineering.

Note: * These Orders are taken direct from price Series published in the *Annual Abstract of Statistics* 1962, Table 362. Order XI is based on leather for footwear, Order II on coal.

(d) *Census Net Output and the Contribution to Gross Domestic Product*

Net output as given in the censuses approximates to the contribution of each industry to Gross Domestic Product; but the two concepts are not identical. Whereas Gross Domestic Product is additive over all sectors of the economy, the contribution of each sector being net of payments due to other industries or sectors, Net Output is only additive within the industrial sector.[1] The net output of each industry therefore does contain certain payments due for services received from firms in non-industrial sectors of

[1] *Guide to Official Sources: No. 6—Census of Production Reports*, H.M.S.O., pp. 15–16.

APPENDIX

the economy. These payments may include repairs, hire of plant, advertising, research work, etc.

According to one official source a reduction of 6 per cent in census net output as published is required to give an approximation to Gross Domestic Product.[1] Adjustments for individual industries varied between 4 and 10 per cent. This, however, was based on 1948 figures for the United Kingdom. For this study the same comparison was made with 1954 figures, and it was found that the net output published in the Census for the United Kingdom required to be reduced by 8 per cent to reconcile with the B.B. figure. If estimates for the repair trades are added to the Census figure a reduction of about 10 per cent is required.

One way of making the appropriate adjustment to the Scottish figures would be to reduce the net output estimates for all years by 10 per cent. Since the estimates have all been adjusted to the 1954 basis, this might be considered a reasonable procedure. In fact it was the method which was tried first. However, the estimates which resulted had some surprising characteristics, especially in 1958 when the Scottish figure seemed to rise faster than might be expected in a year of depression; and if income from employment was subtracted the result was to give 1958 a remarkably high gross trading profit. This method of adjustment therefore seemed too crude.

An alternative procedure was to calculate the relationship between United Kingdom net output and gross product in each year. This required that United Kingdom net output from the various censuses should be adjusted to the 1954 basis as was done for Scotland. When this was done it was found that there was a slight variation in the relationship between net output and gross product. This is shown in Table VI. The table shows that a reduction of 10 per cent as a rough approximation gives reasonable results for most years. But a smaller reduction of about 9 per cent is required in 1951 and 1955; 1957 is only 8 per cent, and 1958 11 per cent. The gross product estimates made by the two methods are very close for 1952, 1953, 1954 and 1956. But the second method gives an increase of £5 million in 1951 and 1955, an increase of £11 million in 1957 and a reduction of £9 million in 1958. Thus a change of one or two per cent in the ratio of net output to gross product can make a very substantial difference to the estimates.

[1] ibid. This is the procedure used for calculating the Index of Industrial Production.

TABLE VI
United Kingdom
G.D.P. in Manufacturing as a Percentage of Adjusted Net Output*

Year	%	Year	%
1951	91·6	1955	90·9
1952	90·1	1956	90·4
1953	89·8	1957	91·6
1954	89·4	1958	88·8

*Including an estimate for repair trades.

Considering the importance of this, the method of adjustment is clearly unsatisfactory. One has to assume not only that the United Kingdom ratio is applicable to Scotland, but that the year to year changes in the United Kingdom ratio are also applicable. For 1959 and 1960 no ratio is available since the Census was not yet published, and a reduction of 10 per cent had to be made on the assumption that it was the best approximation.

In the absence of information relating specifically to Scotland this method of adjustment had to be adopted. An alternative might have been to calculate the United Kingdom ratio of net output to gross product by order groups, and to apply these to the Scottish figures industry by industry to get the effect of the Scottish weighting. This was how the estimates for Northern Ireland were derived.[1] In the Scottish case, however, it seemed unlikely that this procedure would be of much help. The difference between Scotland's industrial structure and that of the United Kingdom is comparatively small as between orders, unlike both Northern Ireland and Wales. The most important differences are concealed within orders. It would be quite impossible to carry out the adjustment at this level.

There is some reason to suppose that the fluctuation in the United Kingdom ratio also applies to Scotland. It will be seen that the years in which the adjustment ratio is smallest, 1951, 1955 and 1957, tend to be boom years, while 1958, the year that it is largest, is a year of depression. It seems a plausible hypothesis that payments for advertising and other services which account for the difference between net output and gross product fluctuate less than the volume of output and therefore make up a larger percentage of net output in depressed years than in times of boom. If this is so, the assumption that the ratio in Scotland fluctuates in the same way as in the United Kingdom may be considered reasonable.

But, of course, even if the fluctuations in the Scottish ratio coincide with those of the United Kingdom, they may be of different proportions. In years of depression, for instance, the change in the ratio may be either greater or less than for the United Kingdom. Unfortunately this cannot be assessed and one has to be content with the application of the United Kingdom ratio year by year, though this is certainly far from satisfactory.

III. CONSTRUCTION

Figures for Building and Contracting published in the 1951 and 1954 Censuses of Production covered only a comparatively small part of the construction industry in Scotland. The 1958 Census gave no figures at all. The best estimate for the whole construction industry in Scotland was published in the Census of Production 1949. The only other published figures of output are for the 'value of work done' (*D.S.S.*); but the earliest year covered by these figures is 1956.

The published material is therefore inadequate. It would be possible to construct estimates for Scotland using these figures if a number of simpli-

---

[1] C. F. Carter and Mary Robson, op. cit.

APPENDIX

fying assumptions are made. First, assuming that the relationship between net output and gross output is the same in Scotland as in the rest of the United Kingdom, a ratio could be derived from the statistics of 'value of work done', which if applied to *B.B.* would give estimates for the period 1956–60. Estimates for the earlier years could be derived from the applications to these figures of the Scottish index of output for the construction industry (Index of Industrial Production (*D.S.S.*)). Adjustment for price changes would have to be made by applying the United Kingdom price index for building and civil engineering. These two indices were applied to the 1956 figure of G.D.P. obtained by the above method, and estimates were thus made for all ten years.

This method, however, relies on two rather weak assumptions: first that a ratio derived from value of work done (or gross output) can be used to obtain net output; and secondly, that adjustment for changes in Scottish prices over the period 1951–56 can be made by applying a United Kingdom price index. Because of these weaknesses it was felt that the estimates derived by this method could not be regarded as satisfactory.

Fortunately it was possible to obtain figures for Schedule E remuneration in the construction industry in Scotland from the Inland Revenue; and with these and the published figures for Schedule D, estimates were built up in a completely different way. Taking Scottish Schedule E income as a proportion of the United Kingdom, the ratio thus derived was applied to income from employment in the United Kingdom (*B.B.*) to give an estimate for Scotland. In the same way the ratio derived from Schedule D was applied to give gross profits and other trading income. These two estimates together gave the contribution to G.D.P.

The figures obtained by both of the above methods are given in Table VII. It is interesting and perhaps a little surprising to see how remarkably close they are. In most years the figures obtained from the tax data method are a little lower than the other estimates, but the difference is small. The estimates obtained by the second method were used since these seemed the most reliable.

IV. TRANSPORT AND COMMUNICATION

This was one of the sectors for which it proved most difficult to make satisfactory estimates. This was chiefly due to the large part played by nationalized industries. These concerns are highly centralized, and it is extremely difficult to obtain regional estimates for their activities which have any meaning at all. It was not possible to make direct estimates of the contribution to G.D.P., instead figures were calculated for income from employment, gross trading profits and gross trading surpluses of public corporations. These three together give the gross product of the industry.

Income from Employment
These estimates were based on Schedule E data supplied by the statistics

TABLE VII
CONSTRUCTION

	1951	1952	1953	1954	1955		1956	1957	1958	1959	1960
METHOD I											
Scottish Production Index (1956=100)	76	80	89	93	94	Value of Work Done Scotland as % of G.B.	9·5	9·9	9·4	9·6	9·4
Price Index (Building & Civil Engineering U.K.) (1956=100)	87	93	91	91	96	Gross Product U.K. (BB) £.m. Northern Ireland £m.	1103 12	1130 13	1183 16	1258 15	1385 17
						Gross Product G.B. £m	1091	1117	1167	1243	1368
Gross Product Scotland	68	77	84	88	93		104	111	110	119	129
METHOD II											
Ratio Scottish Schedule E. Income /U.K.	9·1	9·2	9·5	9·2	9·4		9·2	8·8	8·9	8·7	9·3
Ratio Scottish Schedule D. Income /U.K. Income from	11·0	10·5	10·4	9·7	9·0		9·5	8·0	8·5	8·3	[8·5]*
Employment £m.	50	56	61	66	71		79	79	83	85	99
Gross Trading Profit, etc.	15	15	18	18	18		21	18	21	23	26
Gross Product Scotland	64	71	79	84	89		101	97	104	108	125

APPENDIX

section of the Inland Revenue. The figures supplied gave Railways, Road Transport and Other Transport, Communications and Storage for the years 1950–51 to 1960–61. Shipping was available only for 1960–61.

The shipping figures gave a certain amount of difficulty. Using the 1960–61 figures, Scottish Schedule E income from shipping was only 2 per cent of the United Kingdom figure, while the employment percentage for sea transport was 9·2 (*D.S.S.* and *A.A.S.*). In fact shipping is one of the cases where it is impossible to separate the Schedule E income of the main regions of the United Kingdom and the majority of the income is therefore included under England.[1] It was therefore decided to allocate employment income from shipping by applying the Scottish employment ratio to the United Kingdom figure for Schedule E. By addition a total for employment income in Transport and Communication for Scotland could then be reached which compared with a figure obtained in a similar way from Schedule E statistics for the United Kingdom.

It was found that the United Kingdom figure derived from Schedule E compared very closely indeed with the *B.B.* figures, and such difference as there was could probably be accounted for by the adjustment to calendar years. It would therefore have been possible simply to adjust the Scottish figures to the calendar year basis for final estimates; but it seemed simpler and possibly more accurate to express the figures derived for Scotland as a ratio of the United Kingdom Schedule E figures and to derive final estimates for Scotland by applying this ratio to *B.B.*

Gross Trading Profit

Gross trading profits of companies were derived from Schedule D statistics. This can be unsatisfactory if large concerns based in England and assessed for tax there are operating on any scale in Scotland, But in transport this problem seemed to apply primarily to the nationalized sector. The ratio of Scottish income in Transport and Communication assessed under Schedule D was above 10 per cent of the total United Kingdom income in all years except three.

The United Kingdom was itself short of the *B.B.* figure, because of the differences in the definition of profits. In fact it ranged from 78 per cent of the *B.B.* figure in 1951 to 82 per cent in 1955 and 70 per cent in 1959. No figures under Schedule D were available for 1960.

The final Scottish figures were therefore obtained by applying the Schedule D ratio to the *B.B.* figure for the United Kingdom. The 1960 figure had to be reached by guesswork.[2]

Gross Trading Surpluses

Nationalized concerns play a large part in transport. The British Trans-

[1] See for instance *105th Report of Commissioners of Her Majesty's Inland Revenue*, Appendix II. In this report but not in previous ones, seamen are themselves treated as a separate region.

[2] This problem also arises in the preparation of the *B.B.* estimates for the U.K. (*Sources and Methods*, p. 155.)

port Commission, British Overseas Airways Corporation, British European Airways and the National Dock Labour Board all contribute to the Scottish G.D.P.[1] But since the published accounts do not give regional figures, it is extremely difficult to split up the United Kingdom figures in such a way as to give satisfactory estimates for Scotland. In some cases the difficulty is conceptual as well as practical: one can, for instance, envisage the Scottish region of British railways operating as some sort of entity; but the airlines, B.E.A. and B.O.A.C., are so highly integrated that any attempt to compute the gross trading surplus of these services which accrues specifically to Scotland is bound to be rather meaningless.

The only information which it seemed possible to use was published either in *D.S.S.* or in the financial accounts of the British Transport Commission.[2] From these it was possible to get the Scottish receipts of British Railways (*D.S.S.*) and also certain operating expenses (excluding maintenance) for a number of years (*Annual Accounts*). Scottish receipts for the period 1955–60 averaged about 9·4 per cent of total receipts. The figures for the Welsh study were based on this receipts ratio, but this seemed to be of doubtful validity if expenses formed, as was likely, a larger proportion of total receipts in the region than in the economy as a whole.[3]

The calculation of expenses was complicated and could not be done properly as the British Transport Commission Accounts only gave certain of the expenses by regions. These were given in shillings and pence per train mile. However, it was possible in this way to calculate a substantial part of the working expenses on a regional basis and these would make up the largest part of operating costs according to national accounting definitions. The Scottish share of these expenses came to about 12 per cent of the United Kingdom total. If one then allocated on the same percentage the remaining costs which were not given on a regional basis, notably servicing and cleaning, shunting and administration, a total for costs could be obtained.[4] If this was then subtracted from total receipts, a figure roughly corresponding to trading surplus could be obtained. The Scottish proportion of this figure averaged about 8 per cent.

As regards other forms of transport, certain figures could be obtained from the British Transport Commission Accounts for the Scottish Bus Group, but otherwise regional information was not published. The Scottish Bus Group seemed to play a proportionately larger part in the Scottish economy than buses owned by the Transport Commission in England. Moreover, they made a profit of more than £2 millions in 1961, and with the exclusion of depreciation this might rise possibly to £5 millions. It

[1] The General Post Office is treated as part of the central Government sector being required to hand over to the latter any surpluses it earns and lacking the financial independence of public corporations. *Sources and Methods*, p. 168.

[2] *British Transport Commission*, Annual Report and Accounts.

[3] Edward Nevin (ed.) *The Social Accounts of the Welsh Economy.*

[4] Expenditure on the maintenance of capital equipment was excluded from this calculation.

TABLE VIII

	1950-51	'51-52	'52-53	'53-54	'54-55	'55-56	'56-57	'57-58	'58-59	'59-60	'60-61
						£m.					
Scotland Schedule E Income (excluding shipping)	62	70	70	76	82	87	97	102	100	101	110
Shipping	7	9	9	9	10	11	12	12	11	11	11
TOTAL	69	79	79	85	92	98	109	114	111	112	121
as a % of United Kingdom	9·8	10·0	9·6	9·9	10·0	9·8	10·0	9·8	9·5	9·3	9·2
Scottish Schedule D income as % of U.K. ..	9·5	12·6	12·2	9·9	11·9	11·0	9·3	13·2	10·2	10·3	—

therefore seemed that the part played by the buses counteracted to some extent Scotland's poor showing financially in the railways.

Since information about other activities is entirely lacking, the final estimate was to a great extent a matter of guesswork. It was thought that a ratio of 8 per cent, such as seemed to apply to the railways, would give too low an estimate owing to the part played by other activities, notably the Scottish Bus Group. It was therefore decided to derive Scottish figures by applying a 9 per cent ratio to the *B.B.* figure for the United Kingdom.

The ratio is largely arbitrary, but the results showed Scotland to have a Gross Trading surplus which was in all years except 1960 under £10 millions and in 1958 amounted only to £2 millions. In 1960 the figure was £15 millions, but this was due to the reorganization of the Transport Commission and the payment of a Government subsidy. Since the estimate is so small, it is of little importance whether the ratio should have been 8 per cent or 10 per cent. The effect of such an error on the estimate for transport would be slight and on Gross Domestic Product as a whole, negligible.

V. DISTRIBUTIVE TRADES

This proved to be another sector for which it was difficult to get satisfactory estimates; even the United Kingdom figures leave much to be desired. The *1957 Census of Distribution and Other Services* did not provide figures for Scotland, so that the latest census material relates to 1950.[1] Apart from the lack of figures, however, confusion is apt to arise from the different definitions used for the census, for the National Income Accounts and by the Ministry of Labour (*A.A.S.* and *D.S.S.*). The census and national accounting definitions give a lower employment in manufacturing industry than the Ministry of Labour and a higher employment in Transport and Distribution. For national accounting purposes many of those classified by the Ministry of Labour as employed in manufacturing are regarded as part of Transport or Distribution. In addition to this the adoption of the new Standard Industrial Classification 1958 altered the definition once again. After the change, Ministry of Labour employment figures for Distribution in the United Kingdom increased by about 7 per cent (*A.A.S.*) and the *G.D.P.* estimates (*B.B.*) increased by 2 per cent.

Gross Trading Profit, etc.
The estimation of Gross Trading Profit was the easiest part. This was done on the basis of the Schedule D figures (Inland Revenue Reports), taking the assessments made in a particular year as referring to the profits earned in the previous year. A ratio was derived by comparing Scottish Schedule D income in the Distributive Trades with United Kingdom income, the Scottish figures for Gross Trading Profit were obtained by applying this ratio to the *B.B.* figure. The ratio varied between 8 per cent

[1] *Census of Distribution and Other Services, 1950.*
Census of Distribution and Other Services, 1957.

TABLE IX

Distributive Trades: Inland Revenue Data

	1951	'51-52	'52-53	'53-54	'54-55	'55-56	'56-57	'57-58	'58-59	'59-60	'60-61
Scottish Schedule E Income £m.	56·0	63·1	64·2	67·7	72·2	78·1	84·5	91·8	94·5	100·7	99·5
Scottish Index	100	113	115	121	129	140	151	164	169	180	178
Scotland as % of U.K.	8·1*	8·3	8·1	8·1	7·9	7·8	7·7	7·8	7·6	7·7	7·5
Scottish Sched. D ratio	8·4	8·3	8·5	8·4	8·7	8·6	8·6	9·0	7·9	8·1	[8·1]

*Compared with ratio of 9·1% from Census of Distribution for 1950.

and 9 per cent approximately over the years 1951–59. For 1960 no Schedule D figures were available and the ratio was assumed to remain the same as in 1959. As in other industries the profits assessed under Schedule D were short of the estimates for the United Kingdom in *B.B.* In this case they accounted in most years for over 80 per cent of the latter.

Income from Employment
Figures for income from employment could be derived from Schedule E figures supplied by the Inland Revenue, using these as a ratio of the United Kingdom and applying this to *B.B.* in the same way as for other industries. However, the ratio derived from Schedule E was not compatible with the Census of Distribution figures for 1950. According to the Inland Revenue figures Scottish Schedule E income was 8·1 per cent of the United Kingdom total in 1950–51, while Scottish wages and salaries in the Census of Distribution were 9·1 per cent of the total for Great Britain plus an estimate for Northern Ireland. Furthermore the Inland Revenue figure for total remuneration under Schedule E in Scotland in 1950–51 came to £56 million while the Census of Distribution figure for wages and salaries was £73 million.[1] It was clear that there was a substantial difference in definition; and that the Inland Revenue figures probably followed a similar definition of Distribution to the Ministry of Labour. However, the census figure was not entirely compatible with *B.B.* either, since wages and salaries for Great Britain came to £759 million in 1950 compared with £755 million in *B.B.* for United Kingdom.[2] Despite this, it was clear that the census definition was fairly close to that used in *B.B.* and certainly much closer than the Inland Revenue.

Scottish income from employment in 1950 was therefore derived by applying the ratio of Scottish wages and salaries to those of Great Britain in the census plus an estimate for Northern Ireland. This gave £69 million in 1950. The other years were then obtained by applying the Scottish Schedule E figures as an index to 1950.

VI. INSURANCE, BANKING AND FINANCE

Income from Employment
Income from employment in this group of industries was based on Schedule E statistics, the Scottish figures being supplied by the Inland Revenue Statistics Office. Comparison of earnings assessed under Schedule E for Scotland and for the United Kingdom showed the Scottish proportion varying between 6·6 and 5·5 per cent of the United Kingdom figure. These ratios were then applied to the *B.B.* estimates for the United Kingdom to derive a figure for Scotland.

It appeared that the Schedule E figures for the United Kingdom compared very closely with the *B.B.* estimates, and it is unlikely therefore that

[1] Excluding the repair trades already included with manufacturing.
[2] *National Income and Expenditure, 1958.*

APPENDIX

errors arise out of differences of coverage or definition. For Scotland, however, some error might arise if a significant proportion of those working in Scotland are assessed for tax in England. This is perhaps more likely in these industries than in some others owing to the nature of the firms involved. And it is noteworthy that in 1955 the employment statistics (*D.S.S.*) were revised upwards by 6,000 on the grounds that many employees who had their National Insurance cards held in England were in fact working in Scotland. It is possible that such a discrepancy also arises in the Schedule E figures, and if this is so, the estimates derived for Scotland might be too low.

Gross Profit, Rent, Adjustment for Net Interest
It proved quite impossible to calculate these items separately as is done in *B.B.* The treatment of profits in these industries raises a number of problems owing to the nature of banking income. In the United Kingdom the procedure is to show financial concerns as making a steady annual loss, since the income accruing for financial services rendered is included in the contribution to G.D.P. of those industries receiving the services. If this was attributed to the financial concerns themselves, then it would have to be deducted from each of the other industries. For this reason an item is included in the *B.B.* tables 'adjustment for net interest' to make the contribution of Insurance, Banking and Finance additive with other industries, by excluding that part of the profit which is already contained in the figures for other industries.[1]

There was no basis on which one could make estimates of this nature for Scotland. The Schedule D figures proved to be of no assistance: profits appeared to be negative in some years and positive in others and it seemed impossible to derive any meaningful ratio. In any case many of the firms involved probably have their headquarters in England are not assessed in Scotland for Schedule D.

As a result it was necessary to resort to a rather crude expedient. Gross profit, rent and adjustments for net interest for the United Kingdom were taken together and the Scottish share arrived at on the basis of the employment ratio. Actually the amount of error arising from this procedure is likely to be small, since the absolute amount involved only rises from £7 millions to £15 millions over the period. Therefore, if the ratio is slightly too high or too low, the maximum error involved would be unlikely to exceed £1 million in 1950 or £5 millions in 1960.

The calculation of the employment ratio raises some difficulty owing to the change in definition in 1955. Under the definition used for 1950–54 the ratio averaged 6·5 per cent and for the later period the average was 7·4 per cent. In fact it is the second definition which needs to be used. The earlier figures are therefore grossed up by 19 per cent to allow for this difference. The figures show Scotland to have a diminishing share of total United Kingdom employment in these industries.

[1] *Sources and Methods*, pp. 143 et seq.

An alternative ratio which might have been applied is the Schedule E ratio already used for income from employment. This also fell over the period, but averaged about 6 per cent. The estimates would therefore have been slightly lower if this ratio had been used. In fact there was no reason to suppose that this ratio would produce a more accurate estimate.

TABLE X

Insurance, Banking and Finance

Scotland as % of United Kingdom

	1951	'52	'53	'54	'55	'56	'57	'58	'59	'60
Income assessed under Schedule E	6·6	6·6	6·5	6·3	6·2	6·0	6·2	6·1	5·8	5·5
Employment*	8·0	7·9	8·0	7·5	7·5	7·5	7·6	7·3	7·3	7·3

*Figures for 1950–54 have been adjusted (see text).

VII. OTHER SERVICES

Income from Employment

This group includes Orders XXIII and XXIV of the 1948 Standard Industrial Classification with the exception of public health and education, domestic services and services to non-profit making bodies.[1]

Income assessed under Schedule E for Scotland was obtained from the Inland Revenue Statistics Office for Professional and Scientific Services, Entertainment and Sports, and Other Services. A total was obtained from the United Kingdom Schedule E figures and the Scottish figures were expressed as a proportion. This ratio was then applied to the *B.B.* estimates for the United Kingdom to derive figures for Scotland.

There are some differences in scope between the Schedule E figures and those listed under Other Services in *B.B.*, since the Schedule E figures include some professional services which are listed separately in *B.B.* But the effect of this on the ratio seemed likely to be small and it was felt that the Scottish estimates could be regarded as reasonably accurate.

This was one of the industry groups in which the adoption of the new Standard Industrial Classification made the greatest difference. The *B.B.* estimates for the later years therefore had to be adjusted to pre-1958 definitions.

Gross Trading Profit

Scottish figures were derived by using the ratio of Scottish to United Kingdom income assessed under Schedule D. This was applied to the *B.B.* estimates. As with other industries the income assessed under Schedule D for the United Kingdom was somewhat below the *B.B.* estimates of Gross Trading Profit. In this case Schedule D income varied between 76 and 84 per cent of the latter.

[1] *Sources and Methods*, p. 51.

APPENDIX

TABLE XI

Other Services

	1951	'52	'53	'54	'55	'56	'57	'58	'59	'60
Scotland as % of U.K.										
Total Employment† income as % of U.K. (Schedule E)	9·0	8·9	9·0	8·5	9·3	8·9	8·9	9·1	8·7	8·4
Sched. D income as %² of U.K.	8·7	8·9	8·4	8·4	8·3	8·2	7·9	7·9	7·9	[7·9]*
United Kingdom Income £m.										
B.B. estimates (income from employment)	729	740	752	772	858	963	1,040	1,067‡	1,123‡	1,163‡

* No figure available, 1959 ratio used.
† Tax data refers to tax years.
‡ Adjusted to pre-1958 *B.B.* definitions. Actual *B.B.* figures 1,274; 1,340 and 1,388 for 1958, '59 and '60.

VIII. PUBLIC ADMINISTRATION AND DEFENCE

The income of this group was based on employment statistics. The Inland Revenue figures are of little help, since the majority of all Civil Servants and Armed Forces are assessed centrally and included with the figures for England, no matter which region they happen to be employed in.[1]

Figures are available in *D.S.S.* and *A.A.S.* for civil employment broken down by National and Local Government employees. Scotland had a slightly higher proportion of Local than National Government employees. This could be of some importance since the average earnings for Local Government employees is slightly lower than for National Government employees. The effect of this was worked out by taking average weekly earnings (*Ministry of Labour Gazette*, earnings inquiries) and applying weights to represent both Scottish and United Kingdom employment. It was found that Scotland's distribution of employment on the basis of the same average rates for both Local and National Government employees, caused a reduction of only 0·3 to 0·5 per cent in the combined average earnings.

This, of course, only deals with the effect of a slightly higher proportion of Local Government employees. It assumes that the average earnings rate for Local Government employees and for National Government employees is the same in Scotland as in the United Kingdom as a whole. This may be slightly misleading, but there is no information on which to base an alternative assumption, and it was thought that in this particular group any difference in rates would not be very important.

The estimate for income from civil employment was then made by

[1] See, for instance, *105th Report of the Commissioners of Inland Revenue*.

applying the Scottish employment ratio to the *B.B.* figures and reducing the figure which resulted to take account of Scotland's differing employment distribution.

The estimate for the Armed Forces was made by simply applying the Scottish ratio of employment as shown in *D.S.S.* and *A.A.S.* to the *B.B.* figure. The total estimate for Public Administration and Defence was found to average just over 9 per cent of the *B.B.* figure.

TABLE XII

Public Administration and Defence

	1951	'52	'53	'54	'55	'56	'57	'58	'59	'60
				Scotland as % of U.K.						
Civil Employment	8·6	8·6	8·9	8·7	8·8	8·9	9·0	9·0	8·9	8·7
Armed Forces	9·9	9·7	9·7	10·1	10·1	10·1	10·1	10·3	10·1	10·0

IX. PUBLIC HEALTH SERVICES

Income in this group was estimated mainly from *National Health Service Scotland Acts: Annual Reports* and the *Ministry of Health Annual Reports*.[1] It was possible to add up wages and salaries paid under various headings by the Regional Hospital Board, the Executive Councils and the Dental Board both for Scotland and for England and Wales.

The remuneration of doctors, dentists, pharmacists, ophthalmologists and opticians was not available net of expenses. But it appeared that these incomes were not included in this category anyway but instead formed part of 'Other Services'.

Totalling wages and salaries from the above sources for England, Wales and Scotland, plus an estimate for Northern Ireland, it was found that the figures which resulted were in all cases over 90 per cent of the *B.B.* figure to the nearest calendar year. The Scottish estimate was therefore made by taking the ratio of Scottish wages and salaries to those of the United Kingdom as shown by the accounts and applying this to the *B.B.* estimates. It was found that the Scottish ratio was less than 10 per cent of the United Kingdom in 1951–52 and 1952–53, but was above 10 per cent in other years. The ratio corresponded very closely to Scottish total expenditure on the National Health Service as a proportion of the United Kingdom.

TABLE XIII

Scottish Wages and Salaries in the Public Health Services as % of U.K.

1951-52	'52-53	'53-54	'54-55	'55-56	'56-57	'57-58	'58-59	'59-60	'60-61
9·7	9·6	10·4	10·6	10·8	10·8	10·3	10·6	10·9	11·2

[1] H.M.S.O.

APPENDIX

X. LOCAL AUTHORITY EDUCATIONAL SERVICES

The income of teachers in Scotland was available year by year from *Education in Scotland, Annual Reports*.[1] Figures were also available for the superannuation and national insurance contributions made by authorities on behalf of the educational staff. The figures only required adjustment to a calendar year basis.

Figures for expenditure on 'other salaries and wages', i.e. administration, cleaning, etc. were not available. This had to be estimated by the application of a ratio. The ratio used was the number of pupils in Scottish full time public and grant-aided schools as a proportion of full time pupils in grant-aided and direct grant (but not independent) schools in England and Wales, Scotland and Northern Ireland (*A.A.S., D.S.S.*). This ratio came to about 11 per cent for most years. This was applied to the *B.B.* estimate to give 'other wages and salaries for Scotland'.

Employers' contributions for superannuation and national insurance were likewise only available for the educational staff. An estimate for the others was made on the assumption that employers' contributions for other staff bore the same relation to total employers' contributions as their wages and salaries did to total wages and salaries. This proportion amounted to 17 per cent. Possibly this estimate is slightly misleading, but it ranged only between £0·2 million and £0·6 million.

TABLE XIV

	1951-52	1952	1953	1954	1955	1956	1957	1958	1959	1960
					£ million					
Teachers' salaries	19·0	21·3	22·4	23·9	25·2	28·4	31·5	33·4	36·1	39·0
Other salaries and wages	4·0	4·5	4·6	4·8	5·4	5·9	6·8	7·4	8·2	9·7
Employers' contributions	1·5	1·6	1·8	1·9	2·0	2·5	2·8	3·0	3·4	3·6
	24·5	27·4	28·8	30·6	32·6	36·8	41·1	43·8	47·7	52·3

XI. OWNERSHIP OF DWELLINGS

Income in this category accrues under the following headings:
    (1) Owner occupiers imputed rent
    (2) Private landlord's rent
    (3) Local authority rented houses
    (4) Government owned houses.

The estimates present considerable difficulties even for the United Kingdom.

[1] H.M.S.O., Edinburgh.

Local Authority Housing
This category could be estimated in the same way as for the United Kingdom.[1] Rents accruing to Local Authorities grossly underestimate the value of housing partly because of subsidies and partly because houses are let at rents far below the economic level. The figure used for *B.B.* is therefore the loan charge of Local Authorities as shown in *Local Government Financial Statistics* and *Sources & Methods*, p. 237. This is the loan charge on the capital cost of the housing. Comparable figures are available for Scotland in *Local Government Financial Reports*.[2]

Other Housing
Income from other housing had to be estimated by means of an indicator. That used was income assessed under Schedule A for Scotland as a proportion of the United Kingdom. This averages about 5·7 per cent. The Local Authority housing income for the United Kingdom was subtracted from the *B.B.* total and the indicator applied to allocate the Scottish part of the remainder. Government housing is in effect ignored and treated as if it was part of private housing.

XII. DOMESTIC SERVICES TO HOUSEHOLDS

There was no data for the earnings of domestic servants either by regions or for the United Kingdom other than *B.B.* Figures for employment were available in *A.A.S.* and *D.S.S.*; and the *B.B.* figure for income is therefore apportioned on the basis of the employment ratio.

This is obviously a very rough and ready procedure. It may be that there are substantial regional differences in earnings; and the use of the employment ratio assumes the same earnings per head. Furthermore the number of resident domestic servants as a proportion of the total is much higher in Scotland than in England and Wales. Thus Scotland had less than 10 per cent of the total but more than 10 per cent of resident domestic servants. The Scottish estimate must therefore be regarded as only a rough approximation.

XIII. SERVICES TO PRIVATE NON-PROFIT MAKING BODIES

It was impossible to make a satisfactory estimate of income under this category. No statistics were available either for employment or income. In the inland revenue reports this category is included with Other Services. The procedure adopted was therefore to allocate the Scottish income from the *B.B.* total by applying the ratio of total population in Scotland to that of the United Kingdom. Obviously this is unsatisfactory, but this was the only estimate for which this method had to be used and the amount involved was so small that any error arising from the use of a ratio which was slightly too high or too low would be very small.

[1] *Sources and Methods*, pp. 237 and 337.
[2] H.M.S.O.

APPENDIX

XIV. GROSS DOMESTIC PRODUCT AT CONSTANT PRICES

No information on Scottish prices is available which would make possible a straightforward deflation of the estimates for G.D.P. to give G.D.P. at constant prices. Instead two rather roundabout methods were used neither of which can be considered entirely satisfactory.

For a number of sectors estimates can be derived from the Scottish indices of industrial production (*D.S.S.*). These cover manufacturing, mining and quarrying, gas, electricity and water and construction. Since these are volume indices it should be possible to obtain figures for output at constant prices merely by applying them to the actual figure in the base year (1954). This was the procedure adopted, and in manufacturing especially it is certainly preferable to deflating Scottish output figures by price indices derived from the United Kingdom. But the index of industrial production is intended mainly as an indicator and it is unlikely that it is as accurate as one would wish for this purpose.[1]

For the other sectors the method adopted was to deflate Scottish output at current prices by United Kingdom price indices. The price indices used were all obtained from the figures of gross domestic product at constant and at current prices shown in *B.B.* By dividing the former into the latter one is able to obtain a price index for each sector.

This method is liable to lead to error if price indices for the United Kingdom are unrepresentative of Scottish prices. This would be most likely to arise if the composition of Scottish output in each sector differed from that of the United Kingdom. Manufacturing is, of course, the main sector in which such differences of composition arise, and fortunately it was possible to estimate this sector by the other method. In general it was felt that the use of this second method would not lead to erroneous results in the sectors for which it was used, since these were all fairly similar in Scotland and the United Kingdom. The main exception is probably agriculture, forestry and fishing. Since forestry and fishing play a much larger part in the Scottish total than they do in the rest of the United Kingdom, the use of a United Kingdom price index may be misleading, but there was no other method available.

[1] Especially in view of the questions raised about this index in Chapter 5. This index has now been revised, see footnotes on pp. 35 and 36 and the note on the revised figures on p. 136.

SCOTLAND'S ECONOMIC PROGRESS

PART II

INCOME FROM EMPLOYMENT, GROSS PROFITS AND OTHER TRADING INCOME

(Chapter 3)

FOR a number of industry and service groups the estimates of gross domestic product were compiled from separate totals for income from employment and gross trading profits and other trading income. In such cases the division of gross domestic product into its component parts presented no problem. This applied to construction, transport and communication, the distributive trades, insurance, banking and finance, other services, public administration and defence, public health services, local authority education, ownership of dwellings, domestic services and services to non-profit making bodies.

In agriculture, forestry and fishing separate estimates were made for employment income and profits in forestry and fishing from Schedule E and Schedule D figures used as ratios. In agriculture itself official figures are available for employment income in *Scottish Agricultural Economics*. These were subtracted from the total leaving income from self-employment, gross profits, etc. as a residual.

Estimates for the other industries were made principally from the Censuses of Production; the basic method was therefore to use the official figure for income from employment and derive gross trading profits as a residual after subtracting employment income from gross domestic product. However the process was not as simple as it sounds, since numerous adjustments had to be made to get comparable figures for all years on the same basis as the estimates made for Gross Domestic Product. The years 1959 and 1960 were not covered by the Censuses and a different method had therefore to be used.

(1) *Manufacturing Industry*

As with gross domestic product all the estimates were adjusted to compare with the figures in the 1954 Census. The 1951 estimates comprised large firms only and the total figures therefore had to be increased by 4·3 per cent. The 1958 figures were based on the new Standard Industrial Classification and had to be raised by 7·0 per cent. The sample Censuses of 1955, 1956 and 1957 also gave lower estimates than the full Census of 1954, and the figures for these years had to be increased by 4·5 per cent. These adjustments gave comparative figures on the 1954 basis for 1951, 1954, 1955, 1956, 1957 and 1958. The estimates still did not include those parts of the repair trades excluded from the Census, and to take account of this the estimates all had to be raised by a further 3·0 per cent.

No totals for manufacturing industry in Scotland were published in the sample Censuses of 1952 and 1953. These years therefore presented special problems. The figures for employment income in the published trades made up only 68·2 per cent of the total on the basis of the comparative

APPENDIX

figures for 1951 given in the Censuses. They amounted to only 63·5 of 1951 figures adjusted in the way outlined above. The only available procedure was to gross up the estimates to allow for this difference. This meant increasing the total for the published trades by 57·4 per cent. This rather crude procedure gave estimates for 1952 and 1953 which were then comparable with the other years.

The resulting figures for 1951–58 still did not compare exactly with the income from employment figures in *B.B.* as was shown by a comparison of United Kingdom figures derived from the Censuses with *B.B.* estimates. The principal omission appeared to be employees' superannuation contributions. To allow for this the estimates for all the years 1951 to 1958 were increased by a further 4·5 per cent (the amount of adjustment required for the United Kingdom figures). This gave final estimates for Scotland covering the period 1951–58.[1]

For 1959 and 1960 no Census figures were available. The Inland Revenue supplied figures for 1960–61 but these were based on the revised Standard Industrial Classification and gave a total employment income which even after various adjustments seemed too small. Since comparable 1958 figures were not available it was difficult to make adjustments in a satisfactory manner.

Another possible method was to find the average percentage which employment incomes account for in Gross Domestic Product over the years 1951–58 and to derive figures for 1959 and 1960 by applying this ratio, which averaged 66 per cent, to the Gross Domestic Product figures for 1959 and 1960. This produced estimates of £432 million and £467 million respectively.

But this method seemed to be too crude. Final figures were obtained by estimating income per head and multiplying by the employment figure. Using 1958 as a base it was found that employment income per person employed in the United Kingdom (employees less unemployed) rose from 100 in 1958 to 105·9 in 1959 and 111·2 in 1960. Numerous adjustments had to be made to allow for the change in the Standard Industrial Classification and produce comparable estimates for all three years.

Scottish income per person employed amounted to £578 in 1958 and the application of the index derived from the United Kingdom figure gave an estimate of £612 in 1959 and £642 in 1960. Scottish employment on the other hand fell to 97 per cent of the 1958 level in 1959 and 99·6 per cent in 1960. The final estimates of income from employment therefore came to £438 million in 1959 and £469 million in 1960.

The weak point in this method is the application of the United Kingdom index for income per person employed. But earnings per head tend to keep in step throughout the country, and experience shows that the divergence between rates of increase in Scotland and the rest of the United Kingdom

---

[1] These compare with *National Income and Expenditure, 1958*, and previous years. After 1958 the definition of the U.K. figures is altered to take account of the revised Standard Industrial Classification.

is small over a short period. It therefore seems unlikely that this method would lead to much error. It is noteworthy that the figures are fairly close to those obtained above by applying the simple ratio method to Gross Domestic Product; and it is clear that if the actual figures had been much lower the estimates from gross trading profits, etc. which are obtained by subtraction, would have been surprisingly high.

(2) *Mining and Quarrying*
Estimates for employment income in mining and quarrying were obtained in a similar way to manufacturing. But better figures were available for most years and the process was therefore simpler.

The figure for 1951 was adjusted to the 1954 basis by an increase of 1 per cent to allow for small firms. The figures in the sample Censuses of 1955, 1956 and 1957 were raised by 7·4 per cent and those for 1952 and 1953 by 8·3 per cent. This gave comparable figures for the years 1951 to 1957. All the figures were then adjusted to *B.B.* definitions and to include employers' superannuation contributions. This was done by comparing United Kingdom figures derived from the Census with *B.B.* It involved increases of 5·5 to 6·0 per cent depending on the year.

For 1958 estimates could also be made direct from the Census; but figures for 1958, 1959 and 1960 are extracted from Coal Board data and published in *D.S.S.* It was decided to use these figures and to add to them an estimate for 'other mining and quarrying'. This latter figure amounted to £3·4 million in the 1958 Census and was assumed to rise to £3·5 million in 1959 and £3·6 million in 1960.

(3) *Gas, Electricity and Water*
The same method was used to produce these estimates. The figures in 1951 Census had to be raised by 8·8 per cent to take account of small firms and compare with 1954; 1958 figures were raised by 6·3 per cent. The figures in the sample Censuses likewise needed to be raised, and water undertakings were not included at all. The 1952 and 1953 figures were raised by 20·4 per cent and 1955, 1956 and 1957 by 21·6 per cent. All the figures were then adjusted to include employers' superannuation contributions and to compare with *B.B.*, this involved a further increase of 9 per cent.

Figures for 1959 and 1960 were taken from data in *D.S.S.* This gave totals for wages and salaries including superannuation in gas and electricity. These totals were raised by a further 10 per cent to include income from employment in water undertakings. This percentage adjustment was estimated from the income from employment in water undertakings in the 1958 Census.

(4) *Income from Self-Employment* (Chapter 3, Table VI)
Income from self-employment was obtained from the Schedule D figures in the *Inland Revenue Reports*. The reports give figures for Schedule

APPENDIX

D income of 'sole traders and partnerships in Scotland', which was taken as the equivalent of self-employment. Unlike companies whose branches in regions of the United Kingdom may be assessed centrally for tax, it was considered unlikely that there would be much discrepancy between the place of work and place of assessment.

The income of sole-traders and partnerships in Scotland was expressed as a percentage of the United Kingdom total and applied to the figures for income from self-employment in *B.B.* to get totals for Scotland. Subtraction of these totals from the estimates in Chapter 3, Table I, gave a residual comprising gross profits of companies, gross surpluses of public corporations and rent.

Gross profits of 'Scottish' companies and local authorities, meaning by this companies having their headquarters in Scotland, were assumed equivalent to the profits of those companies assessed for tax in Scotland. These figures were also obtained from the Schedule D figures in the *Inland Revenue Reports*.

SCOTLAND'S ECONOMIC PROGRESS

PART III

INVESTMENT

(Chapter 9)

(1) *Fixed Investment in Manufacturing Industry 1951–60*
Almost all of the estimates were derived from the Censuses of Production and the main problem was to obtain comparable figures for all the years covered. Adjustments had to be made to the figures published in the censuses to make comparisons possible for the same reasons as already outlined earlier in this Appendix. As with all other estimates the investment figures were adjusted to compare with those given in the 1954 Census. This meant that the 1951 figures had to be increased to include small firms; 1958 figures had to be adjusted for the change in Standard Industrial Classification; and the figures taken from sample Censuses, 1952, 1953, 1955, 1956 and 1957 had to be revised upwards to compare with the wider scope of the full Census in 1954. For this reason the figures given in Table I (Chapter 9) differ slightly from those published in the report of the Toothill Committee which were taken direct from the sample census and did not include estimates for all of the years covered here.[1]

For Scotland these adjustments amounted to an increase of 1·8 per cent on the 1951 figure for large establishments; an increase of 2·9 per cent on the 1958 figure; and increases of 4·2 per cent for the years 1955, 1956 and 1957. For 1952 and 1953 much more serious problems arose, since the sample censuses of these years gave no totals for manufacturing industries as a whole. The sum of the figures for the published trades gave a figure which was far short of the total. Comparative figures were, however, available for 1951; and on the basis of these the totals for all the published trades in 1952 and 1953 were increased by 89 per cent to get an estimate for manufacturing industry as a whole. The estimates for these years are therefore much weaker than the remainder, but without them it would have been impossible to make any continuous analysis before 1954.

Scottish figures for 1959 and 1960 were not available from any Government publication at the time of writing, but fortunately estimates were prepared for the Toothill Committee and are published in their report.[2]

The Welsh figures were obtained by similar methods to those used for Scotland. For 1952 and 1953, however, figures were available in Nevin's *Social Accounts of the Welsh Economy*.[3] These figures were used, although Nevin's figures for other years differ considerably from those published in the Censuses and their reliability is therefore open to question. For 1959

---

[1] *Report on the Scottish Economy*, Scottish Council, 1961, p. 42.
[2] Ibid., p. 43.
[3] *Social Accounts of the Welsh Economy*, No. 2, University of Wales Press, 1957, p. 12.

APPENDIX

and 1960 Welsh figures were available from the *Digest of Welsh Statistics*.[1]

For Northern Ireland and the United Kingdom the figures were better and more readily obtained. The Northern Ireland figures were all taken from Censuses of Production for Northern Ireland which gave figures for all years and were published up to 1960 at the time of writing. United Kingdom figures were likewise taken from the Censuses of Production except for 1959 and 1960 when Census data published in *A.A.S.* was used. As for Scotland and Wales, United Kingdom figures had to be adjusted for the change in the Standard Industrial Classification and adjustments also had to be made to the figures obtained from the sample Censuses.

Investment in Manufacturing Industry at 1954 Prices (Table II)
The indices used in this table were constructed by applying a price index as a deflator to the figures for investment at current prices. The price index was calculated by dividing the United Kingdom figures for investment at current prices by those for investment at constant prices both of which are given in *B.B.*[2] The index was then applied to the figures of investment at current prices for Scotland, Wales and Northern Ireland to get investment at constant prices. This procedure may be misleading if the United Kingdom price index does not accord with the actual price changes of investment in Scotland, Wales and Northern Ireland. No doubt some error may arise in this way; but it was thought that the method would give reasonable results and that regional prices of investment goods would certainly keep more closely in step than the prices of manufacturing output as a whole.

Price Index of Capital Formation in Manufacturing

1951	1952	1953	1954	1955	1956	1957	1958	1959	1960
86·8	97·1	99·4	100	105·3	111·9	117·2	121·0	120·5	121·5

[1] *Digest of Welsh Statistics*, No. 8, 1961, H.M.S.O. (Table 39).
[2] *National Income and Expenditure, 1962* (Table 56).

INDEX

Agriculture, 24–36, 38–46, 90, 140–3, 172
Alcoholic drink, expenditure on, 90–8 *passim*, 122
Armed forces, 168
Attwood, E. A., and Geary, R. C., *Irish County Incomes*, 86–7

Beacham, A., 107
Belgium, 22
Bricks, pottery and glass industries, 53–6, 60, 104, 143–56 *passim*
British Transport Commission, 160–2

Cairncross, A. K., 15n, 106n
Campbell, A. D., 15, 18, 21, 72, 139, 140
Capital/output ratios, 106–18 *passim*
Carter, C. F., and Robson, M., 15, 18, 19, 34n, 139, 156
Census of Distribution, 162–4
Census of Production, 14, 15, 17, 26, 41n, 44n, 50, 52–6 *passim*, 58–9, 64, 99–100, 107, 115, 140, 143–57, 172–7
— of Northern Ireland, 14, 39, 55, 56, 58
Central Scotland: A Programme for Development and Growth, Cmnd. 2188, 13, 127, 129, 131
Chemicals, 48–56, 61–3, 101, 104, 143–56 *passim*
Clothing, expenditure on, 90–8 *passim*
— and footwear industries, 48–56, 101, 104, 143–56 *passim*
Clydeside conurbation, 81–9 *passim*, 122
Coal, *see* Mining and quarrying
Construction, 25–36 *passim*, 38, 47, 132–5, 156–7
Crofting, 26
Cuthbert, N. (Isles and Cuthbert, *Economic Survey of Northern Ireland*), 15, 71n, 139, 140

Deane, Phyllis, 67
Denmark, 22
Depreciation, 39, 40, 141
Distribution, 25–36, 38–45, 47, 162–4

East and West Ridings Region, 66–80, 90, 98
Eastern Region, 66–80, 90–98
Economic structure, Scotland compared with U.K. and other regions, 24–7, 48–9, 57, 101, 121, 125, 132
Education, 24–36 *passim*, 105, 169
Emigration, 23, 129–30
Employment statistics, 146, 148, 162
Engineering and electrical industries, 48–56, 101, 104, 117, 143–56 *passim*
Europe, comparison of living standards, 21–2

Fishing, 24–36, 38–46, 140–3, 172
Food, drink and tobacco, 48–56, 61–3, 104, 143–56 *passim*
Forestry, 24–36, 38–46, 140–3, 172
Fuel and light, 90–8 *passim*

Gas, electricity and water, 26–36, 39–45, 99–102, 105, 143–56, 174
Geary, R. C., *see* Attwood, E. A.
Germany (West), 22, 28, 101, 106
Gilbert, M., and Associates, *Comparative National Products and Price Levels*, 22
Glovemaking, 146–7
Growth, rates of, 27–30, 35–6, 47, 49–50, 106–18, 119–24, 129 f.
Guide to Official Sources. Census of Production Reports, 144, 154

Hall Report (*Report of Joint Working Party on the Economy of Northern Ireland*), 13
Health Services, 24–36 *passim*, 99, 105, 168
Housing, 90–8 *passim*, 99, 102, 105, 122, 169–70
— (house mortgage outlays), 94

Income, personal, 66–89, 92–3, 120–2
— from employment, 37–46, 66–89 *passim*, 120, 156–75
— per employee, 38–9, 44, 74, 80, 120
— from investment, 71 f., 81f., 91
— from property, 71 f., 82 f.

INDEX

Income, distinction between income arising within and accruing to a region, 67, 86–7
— distribution of, 69
— from other regions and abroad, 70, 126
— tax, 91, 122
Index of Industrial Production, Scotland, 14, 15, 27–8, 36n, 57, 65, 108, 115, 119–23, 124, 143, 151–5 *passim*, 157
— Revision of, *Preface*, 28n, 49n, 109n, 112n, 116n, 120n, 121n
— Northern Ireland, 15, 57–65, 108
Industrial structure, *see* Economic structure
Inflation, in Scotland compared with U.K., 27, 57–65, 107–8, 121
Inland Revenue, *Preface*, 14, 18, 40, 41, 46, 66–89 *passim*, 139–43 *passim*, 156–75 *passim*
Insurance, banking and finance, 26–36, 42–4, 47, 164–6
Investment, 18, 39, 94–5, 99–118, 122, 125, 131, 135, 176–7
— distinction between net and gross, 110–11
Ireland, Northern, Estimate of G.D.P., *Preface*, 15, 23–36, 124
— statistics, 14–16
— personal income, 66–80, 122
— expenditure, 90–8
— investment, 99–118, 176–7
— index of industrial production, 15, 57–65, 108
— *see also* Hall Report
— Republic of, 22, 28, 86–7
Isles, K. S., *see* Cuthbert, N.
Italy, 22, 28, 106

Lamfalussy, A., 22, 106, 111, 113n, 114, 117n
Lewis, J. Parry, 15, 16n
Leather industries, 53–6, 60, 104, 143–56 *passim*

Manufacturing industry, 24–36 *passim*, 37–45, 47–65, 99–118, 121, 143–56, 172–4
Metal goods industries, 53–6, 60, 104, 143–56 *passim*

Metal manufacture, 39, 48–56, 61–4, 101, 104, 143–56 *passim*
Midland Region, 13, 66–80, 90–8
Mining and quarrying, 24–36 *passim*, 99, 102, 105, 131, 143–56, 174.
Ministry of Labour, 17, 38, 162
— *Expenditure Inquiries*, 90, 96–8
— *Statistics on Income, Prices, Employment and Production*, 14n
Multiplier, 126–7, 134

National Income Statistics: Sources and Methods, 139–71 *passim*
Netherlands, 22
Nevin, E. T., *The Social Accounts of the Welsh Economy*, 15, 16, 18, 34n, 44n, 99, 107, 160, 176
Non-metalliferous mining products, etc., *see* Bricks, pottery and glass industries
Northern Region, 66–80, 90–8
— *The North-East, A Programme for Development and Growth*, Cmnd, 2206, 13, 127, 129, 131
North Midland Region, 66–80, 90–8
North-West Region, 66–80, 90–8
Norway, 22

Other services, 166–7
Output, per head, 20–36 *passim*, 50–2, 56
— distinction between net output and contribution to G.D.P., 154–6
— distinction between net output and gross output, 64, 157
Ownership of dwellings, 26–36, 169–70

Participation, level of, 23, 73, 79, 129–30, 133
Paper, printing and publishing, 48–56, 101, 104, 143–56 *passim*
Post Office, 160n
Precision instruments, 53, 145, 146, 151
Prices, 57–65, 108, 121, 151–4, 157, 171, 177
Productivity, 23–7 *passim*, 32–4, 47, 50–2, 56, 120, 121, 129–31
— related to investment, 115–17, 123
Profits, 37–47, 71 f., 81–9 *passim*, 120, 139, 143, 157–67 *passim*, 172–5

INDEX

Property, income from, 71 f., 82 f.
Public administration and defence, 24 f., 39, 42–4, 167–8

Railways, 160–2
Registrar-General, Report of, 81, 88–9n
Rent, 39, 41, 141, 165, 169
Repair trades, 54, 147–9
Roads, 99, 105

Salaries, 52, 56, 71 f., 143
Saving, 72, 92–5, 122, 126–7
Seamen, income of, 67, 68, 77 f.
Self-employment, income from, 39–41, 45–6, 120, 174–5
Shipbuilding and marine engineering, 48–56, 61–4, 104, 117, 131, 132, 143–56 *passim*
State mines and quarries, 147
Social Accounts of the Welsh Economy, see Nevin, E. T.
South-East Region, 13, 66–80, 86, 90–8, 122
Southern Region, 66–80, 90–8
South-West Region, 66–80, 90–8, 122
Standard Industrial Classification, change in, 17, 144, 148, 150, 173
Standard of living, Scotland compared with other areas, 21 f., 117
Stock appreciation, 20, 31
Sweden, 22

Switzerland, 22

Textiles, 39, 48–56, 61–3, 101, 104, 117, 143–56 *passim*
Thomas, Brinley, 16n
Timber and furniture industries, 48–56, 61–3, 104, 143–56 *passim*
Tobacco, expenditure on, 90–8 *passim*, 122
Toothill Report (*Report of the Committee of Inquiry into the Scottish Economy*), 13, 48, 99, 129, 131
Trade cycle fluctuations, 21
Training, 134
Transport, expenditure on, 90–8
Transport and communications, 24–36 *passim*, 47, 148, 157–62

Undisclosed trades, 145–9
Unemployment, 23, 73, 79, 123, 129–31, 133–5

Vehicles, 48–56, 61, 104, 143–56 *passim*

Wages, 37, 52, 143
Wales, estimates of G.D.P., 15–16, 23–36
— personal income, 66–80, 122
— expenditure, 90–8
— investment, 99–118, 176–7
Wood and cork industries, see Timber
Working population, 23, 27

For Product Safety Concerns and Information please contact our EU
representative GPSR@taylorandfrancis.com
Taylor & Francis Verlag GmbH, Kaufingerstraße 24, 80331 München, Germany

www.ingramcontent.com/pod-product-compliance
Lightning Source LLC
Chambersburg PA
CBHW070616300426
44113CB00010B/1546